SARAH ORNE JEWETT

LETTERS OF
SARAH ORNE JEWETT

EDITED BY

ANNIE FIELDS

BOSTON AND NEW YORK
HOUGHTON MIFFLIN COMPANY
The Riverside Press Cambridge
1911

NOTE

THE EDITOR regrets that a friendly message from Mr. William Dean Howells offering letters from Miss Jewett for publication arrived too late to insert them in these pages.

LETTERS

For Lovers' eyes more sharply-sighted be
Than other men's, and in dear Love's delight
See more than any other eyes can see.

. . . .

But they who love indeed, look otherwise
With pure regard and spotless true intent,
Drawing out of the object of their eyes
A more refinèd form which they present.

. . . .

Love thereon fixeth all his fantasie,
And fully setteth his felicitie,
Counting it fairer than it is indeed,
And yet indeed its fairness doth exceed!
Spenser's Hymn in Honour of Beauty.

LETTERS OF SARAH ORNE JEWETT

IN the village of South Berwick, Maine, which had always been Miss Jewett's home, she died June 24, 1909. This village has been no exception to the changes inevitably advancing in the life of small towns in New England. The immediate vicinities of villages are becoming more beautiful, more developed, day by day, while the encroachment of manufacturing, especially where there are full flowing water-courses, brings multitudes of mill people into the heart of the little towns, and as the old English descendants die out, they are naturally replaced by men, women, and children, who can run the manufactories. Formerly Berwick was in the "deestrict" of Maine, as Lowell loved to call it. Portsmouth then seemed the capital of New England and the governors and clergymen thereof were rulers and potentates, bending the knee only to the King of the Fatherland and the great God in Heaven; and Berwick was not far from Portsmouth, even in those days. The beautiful river Piscataqua swept good-sized vessels up to the very banks of the village. Here, and among these descendants, Sarah Orne Jewett grew up with hills and waters and a large open country all about her. This wild land she knew and loved well, as her books show.

She was born September 3, 1849, going to the village school and later to the Berwick Academy, and to both rather intermittently, being but a delicate child. Her father was a physician, and when the weather was pleasant he would take his wise little girl into the chaise by his side in the morning, instead of urging her to go to school. These days, out in the open country with her father, became the white mile-stones of her life. In every house where they stopped she knew the people were her father's friends. When she was tired sitting in the chaise, during his long visits, she would climb down and play about the green dooryards by herself, unless some member of the household happened to see her and call her from the side door to give her a bit of gingerbread, saved or made for the doctor's child. Those were happy and never-to-be-forgotten days. But I fear there were days when father, as well as child, was torn between the happiness of such mornings and duty to the school.

As she grew older her interest in her father's work developed, and she began to question him. Little by little, as he found she could understand and remember what he told her, he would give her larger and deeper lessons, until many a young graduating doctor today might well envy that slip of a girl for the knowledge at first hand which had been conveyed to her impressionable mind. After her father's early death she loved to go into his office to consult his diary; she knew his papers, his books, his medicines, — nothing that belonged to his mind or his work was foreign to her.

Her father's intelligent companionship is made clear to us in her published work. With his death came her first sorrow, —

" The first of all her dead that were to be " ;

and soon after began the correspondence contained in this volume. It is a diary in truth and almost unconsciously; reminding one by its lightness of touch of the famous journal of Dean Swift to Stella, two hundred years ago. The same handling of "the little language" is here ; the same joy and repose in friendship.

This "little language," the private "cuddling" of lovers, of mothers, and children, since the world began, was native also to her. They are the letters, too, of a true lover of nature and of one accustomed to tender communings with woods and streams, with the garden and the bright air. She was no recluse, and loved her world of friends and was a brave spirit among them; using herself to the top of her bent in spite of trammelings of ill health. To one who seldom if ever knew the joy of springing early from her bed, with the thought of a new day, life was contracted and hampered; but in the hours of health allowed her, it was enjoyed with the chastened spirit of one who already knew the sufferings of others and could sympathize with their disabilities. She disliked profoundly all talk of illness and complaining, and demanded no sympathy; but her inherited love of helping the unfortunate led her to study methods of relief, and if she had been a strong person she would have studied medicine in the medical schools. As it was, her gift was undeniable, and the physicians of her acquaintance have borne testimony to her instinctive power of discernment and helpfulness.

Many years later, in 1893, when an illustrated edition of her first book, "Deephaven," was published, we find affixed to the volume a new preface which contains some of her very best and most autobiographical writing. After speaking of the changes creeping over the old village life and the many excellent reasons therefor, she says: "Old farmhouses opened their doors to the cheerful gayety of summer; the old jokes about the respective aggressions and ignorances of city and country cousins gave place to new compliments between the summer boarder and his rustic host. The young writer of these Deephaven sketches was possessed by a dark fear that townspeople and country people would never understand one another, or learn to profit by their new relationship. It seemed not altogether reasonable when timid ladies mistook a selectman for a tramp, because he happened to be crossing a field in his shirt-sleeves. At the same time, she was sensible of grave wrong and misunderstanding when these same timid ladies were regarded with suspicion, and their kindnesses were believed to come from pride and patronage. There is a noble saying of Plato that the best thing that can be done for the

people of a state is to make them acquainted
with one another. It was happily in the writer's childhood that Mrs. Stowe had written of
those who dwelt along the wooded seacoast
and by the decaying, shipless harbors of Maine.
The first chapters of 'The Pearl of Orr's
Island' gave the young author of 'Deephaven' to see with new eyes, and to follow
eagerly the old shore-paths from one gray,
weather-beaten house to another, where Genius
pointed her the way. . . . There will also exist,"
Miss Jewett continues, "that other class of
country people who preserve the best traditions of culture and of manners, from some
divine inborn instinct toward what is simplest
and best and purest, who know the best because they themselves are of kin to it. Human
nature is the same the world over, provincial
and rustic influences must ever produce much
the same effects upon character, and town life
will ever have in its gift the spirit of the present, while it may take again from the quiet
of the hills and fields and the conservatism of
country hearts a gift from the spirit of the
past."

If the high end and purpose of her work
gave her joy, so also did the recognition of it

by others on the way give her pleasure; as
when T. B. Aldrich once wrote : " A great
many thanks for your very kind note about
the July ' Atlantic.' Whenever you give me
one of your perfect little stories the whole
number seems in bloom ! " A letter, too, from
Rudyard Kipling gave her unending pleasure,
in which he says, speaking of the " Country
of the Pointed Firs" : "I am writing to you
to convey some small instalment of our satisfaction in that perfect little tale. It 's immense
— it is the very life. So many of the people
of lesser sympathy have missed the lovely
New England landscape, and the genuine New
England nature." He adds jovially in the
postscript, "I don't believe even you know
how good that work is."

A certain sweet dignity of character dis-
tinguished Miss Jewett; one which never put
a barrier between her and any one else, but
was a part of her very self; with all her wit
and humor and kind ways there was no suggestion leading to sudden nearness nor too
great intimacy.

Her *métier* was, to lay open, for other eyes
to see, those qualities in human nature which
ennoble their possessors, high or low, rich or

poor; those floods of sympathy to be unsealed in the most unpromising and dusty natures by the touch of a divining spirit. Finding herself in some dim way the owner of this sacred touchstone, what wonder that she loved her work and believed in it?

After a severe carriage accident once, she wrote to me: " I was strongly tempted to say yes about Wednesday. . . . I long to see you more than I can say, but I am almost afraid to make a break just now lest I could n't get going again, and there are three chapters at least that I *must* get done before I feel really certain about anything. When I have them safe landed like little fishes, I can take my time. Oh, if I can only get this work done so that you will be pleased and a little proud about it, it seems to me that I shall ask for nothing more. I am so afraid that I can't give it breadth and largeness enough, and that it will have a dull kind of excellence and not real life and vitality."

She was not born to a large city and was unaccustomed to public business and stir, but she was always ready to do what she could. When meetings of societies were called in the village, and Miss Jewett was asked to receive

two or three delegates as guests, she was always
glad to do so. She interrupts one of her notes
to say : —

"I must look sharp after Miss Rickett and
the rest. They were at their meetings all day
yesterday, getting home in the evening at
eleven at night, or a few minutes before, but
they would not like to be called dissipated, I
am sure."

Her eagerness to make life a little easier for
others was always on the alert, as when she
burst out in one of her notes : " Oh, do let us
always *tell* people when we like their work—
it does do so much good." Mrs. Meynell,
writing of Miss Jewett, in a late letter, says :
"I always thought of her as the most selfless
creature I had ever known ; a few hours in
her dear company convinced me of that ; and
her letters are inevitably like her."

But these fragments from her letters carry
us too far afield. They shall be given freely in
the following pages, in order to show her life
as in a mirror, while the days sped on. They
will show, above all, the portrait of a friend
and the power that lies in friendship to sus-
tain the giver as well as the receiver. They
are in the easy undress of every-day life, wear-

ing a grace which lies beyond all thought
of the larger world.

(TO MRS. FIELDS)

LITTLE COMPTON, R. I., 8 *September*, 1880.

DEAR MRS. FIELDS, — This is not a land
where it is easy to write letters. I can't help
being idle, except in thought, and I think I
never knew so quiet a country. It is all like
the places one goes to on the way to sleep.
There are n't any high hills, but you look over
the fields which are so like moors, and you
look and look, and there is nothing you have
to stop and wonder about, the big round-
headed windmills are all still, and today is a
grey day which can't make up its mind to
take the trouble to rain, and here we are sitting by the fireplace, and I was busy watching the smoke until I thought I would write a
letter or two. And whether I drive or sail I
am the most placid and serene of all your
friends, and I forget that I ever was a girl
who could n't go to sleep at night.

After this first letter the days passed without any record which has been preserved, until

bits of diary occur written during her life at
South Berwick in the following years.

"The country is beautiful to look at, but
it is such clear cold weather that you feel as
if you were under a great block of clear, shining ice, instead of air and sky. There is a
grey cloud-bank hanging over the sea all along
the eastern horizon and I think it is going to
snow again, or rain. The wood-sleds are creeping out of the woods and into the village, and
the oxen are like rocks from the pastures, or
the tops of ledges, they look so hard and
tough and frosted over.

You are like my monkey and the jack-in-
the-box with your meetings. Some day you
will get up a big one that will scare you to
death."

Tuesday, 1882.

I hate to keep sending you letters instead
of going to you myself, but by and by there
will be no letters at all. Your little word of
last night has just come and I wish I were
going to be there to welcome you home from
the perils of Bridgewater.[1] It is a hot, tire-

[1] Bridgewater State Farm, which was then a most unpala-
table place.

some day, and I did not get up until very late,
and what book do you think I read in bed?
A hand-book of Anatomy, and I found it very
interesting. Sometimes I think I should like
to give up the world, the f—, and the d—,
and be a doctor, though very likely I am
enough of one already to get the best of it
for myself, and perhaps I have done as much
as I ever could for other people.

Saturday morning, 1882.

I have just seen the notice of Longfellow's
death, and while it was hardly a surprise, still
it gave me a great shock. Are not you glad
that we saw him on that pleasant day when
he was ready to talk about books and people,
and showed so few signs of the weakness and
pain which troubled us in those other visits?
It will always be a most delightful memory,
and it is all the better that we did not dream
it was your last good-bye. I can't help saying
that I am glad he has gone away before you
had to leave him and know it was the last
time you should see him. I dreaded your getting the news of this after we were on the other
side of the sea, darling! After all, it is change
that is so hard to bear, change grows every

year a harder part of our losses. It is fitting
over our old selves to new conditions of things,
without the help of the ones who made it
easier for us to live, and to do our best that
is so hard! I have just been thinking that a
life like that is so much less affected by death
than most lives. A man who has written as
Longfellow wrote, stays in this world always
to be known and loved — to be a helper and
a friend to his fellow men. It is a grander
thing than we can wholly grasp, that life of
his, a wonderful life, that is not shut in to
his own household or kept to the limits of his
every-day existence. That part of him seems
very little when one measures the rest of him
with it, and the possibilities of this imperfect
world reach out to a wide horizon, for one's
eye cannot follow the roads his thought and
influence have always gone. And now what
must heaven be to him! This world could
hardly ask any more from him : he has done
so much for it, and the news of his death
takes away from most people nothing of his
life. His work stands like a great cathedral
in which the world may worship and be taught
to pray, long after its tired architect goes
home to rest.

I cannot help thinking of those fatherless daughters of his. I know they were glad and proud because he was famous and everybody honored him, and they are being told those things over and over in these days, and are not comforted. Only one's own faith and bravery help one to live at first.

March 24.

Today is father's birthday. I wonder if people keep the day they die for another birthday after they get to heaven ? I have been thinking about him a very great deal this last day or two. I wonder if I am doing at all the things he wishes I would do, and I hope he does not get tired of me.

After a long season, passed chiefly in England and France, Miss Jewett wrote from South Berwick in the autumn: —

Thursday, 6 October, 1882.

Here I am at the desk again, all as natural as can be and writing a first letter to you with so much love, and remembering that this is the first morning in more than seven months that I have n't waked up to hear your dear voice and see your dear face. I do miss it very much, but I look forward to no long separation, which is a comfort. It was lovely in the old house and I did so wish you had come down, too, it was all so sweet and full of welcome, and Hannah and Annie and John and Hilborn and Lizzie Pray all in *such* a state because I had got home !

[1883.]

I shall be with you tomorrow, your dear birthday. How I am looking forward to Thursday evening. I don't care whether there is starlight or a fog. Yes, dear, I will bring the last sketch and give it its last touches if you think I had better spend any more time on it. I am tired of writing things. I want now to paint things, and drive things, and *kiss* things, and yet I have been thinking all day what a lovely sketch it would be to tell the story of the day we went to Morwenstow, with bits of "Lorna Doone" and "The Vicar" intertwined with the narrative.

I have been reading Carlyle's Reminiscences — the Jane Welsh Carlyle, as you may suppose. How could people have made such a fuss about it. It seems to grow more and more simple and beautiful and human, and Carlyle is like a "great stone face" on a mountain

top. Good-night, and God bless you, dear
love.

Monday evening, 1883.

Today I have been reading hard, in Thierry
chiefly, with some other big books alongside,
and I feel as if I had been over-eating with
my head! ! ! I try to think how fortunate it
is that I should be well paid for learning a
thing that I ought to know at any rate, but
all that period is very difficult for any one to
straighten out who has not been a student of
history. It is so important and such a key-note
to later English history, that I think of the
early Britons all sound asleep under the green
grass of Salisbury Plain, and feel as if they
would have been quite within my grasp! When
I read the " Saturday Review " and " Spectator " I find myself calling one politician a
Saxon and the next a Norman! Indeed I can
pick them out here in Berwick!

The wet weather has kept us in, but we did
manage to get a drive yesterday among the
green fields and trees. Do you think the
country ever looked so lovely as it does this
summer? I seem to have brought new eyes
home from last year's travels! My mind is

vexed with "Clarissa Harlowe." Zola is not half so unpleasant, we are not worse, but better, when he writes as he does and we read. But the shrewdness of workmanship, the clever maintenance of interest are amazing. It fools my mind in a way that naughty books of the French sort never do. So much for Clarissa, a person of many misfortunes, but I learn a good deal and profit much from the old novel, it accounts for so much in literary traditions.

Sunday, 24 *June.*

DEAREST, — More than once I have really been with you on the piazza, looking out to sea, but the rest of me was here in church, waiting for a very long sermon to be done. It was such an old-fashioned discourse that it "carried me back" more than it is likely to carry me forward, I fear. I don't know who the old minister was, but the day is so hot that the congregation was a very sleepy one.

I am thinking and planning my stories over and over, and first of all seems to come the gray man. It was very funny; I had the solitary man whom I talked about at first, and then came the "man who never smiled," and I coquetted over these two estimable charac-

ters for some days, when suddenly without
note or warning they turned a double somer-
sault and one swallowed the other, and I found
they were really one person! The Gray Man
was masquerading a little, that was all, and
by this time I have ever so many notes about
him and I long to write him all down before
I see you again.

Sunday evening.

I wonder if your pine boughs smell as sweet
as mine tonight? Also I wonder if it is going
to rain! I went to church this morning, and
have been reading all the afternoon, chiefly
the last volume of Dickens' Letters, and I
thought of you at every turn. What a lovely
spirit there is in them! I think his letters to
his sons, as they went away to the army or
to Australia, are wonderfully beautiful. It
was good to have the book fresh in my mind
again. Now, dear, I have at last, after much
grumbling and groaning, got my next two
numbers of the "Marsh Island" ready for
the printer, and I take a long breath, being
free until February. The second of the two
was not half so bad as I expected, and some
day or two in town will work wonders with

the rest. If I had another week I would write the McClure story, and what a triumphant Pinny[1] that would be, ladies.

Mother is reading the Parson Hawker book, with seeming joy, and I don't think she will mind in the least being left alone. I begin to feel dreadfully confused about Christmas now that the story is off my mind for a little while, but we shall soon talk about things, shan't we? and in this next week I shall come quite to my senses.

Does Sandpiper[2] play with you, or has she married a ghost and therefore she cannot come? (Marigold being "excused" on account of following after Clark and Brown's Oxen.) Did you see the interview with "thy friend"[3] and the remark that the best parlor was stiff and prim? I think that was quite an unnecessary comment, but a very observing interviewer, ladies.

I wonder how far you have got in the Swedenborg book? I keep a sense of it under

[1] She was called "'Pinny,' Ladies," she once wrote, "because she was so straight and thin and her head no bigger than a pin's."

[2] Her pet name for Celia Thaxter.

[3] Whittier.

everything else. How such a bit of foundation lifts up all one's other thoughts together, and makes us feel as if we really stood higher and could see more of the world. I am going to hunt up some of the smaller books of extracts, etc., that Professor Parsons gave me. Oh! the garden is so splendid! I never dreamed of so many hollyhocks in a double row and all my own!

Thursday night, 1884.

This morning I read Mr. Arnold's "Nineteenth Century" paper with great joy. What a great man he is! That holds the truth of the matter if anything does. It is all very well to say, as Mr. Blaine does, "What business has England?" The association of different peoples is after all beyond human control: we are "mixed and sorted" by a higher power. And looked at from the human side, what business has one nation to keep another under her authority, but the business of the stronger keeping the weaker in check when the weaker is an enemy? It had to be settled between England and Ireland certainly—for the two races were antagonistic, and England could not have said "no matter, she may plague me and fight me as she pleases." Law

and order come in, and Ireland has a right to
complain of being badly governed, — so has a
child or any irresponsible person, but we can't
question the fact that they must be governed.
Ireland is backward, and when she is equal to
being independent, and free to make her own
laws, I suppose the way will be opened, and
she will be under grace of herself, instead of
tutors and governors in England. Everybody
who studies the case, as Mr. Arnold has, be-
lieves that she must still be governed. I don't
grow very sentimental about Ireland's past
wrongs and miseries. If we look into the history of any subject country, or indeed of any
country at all, the suffering is more likely to
be extreme that length of time ago, and I
think as Mr. Arnold does, and as Mr. Lowell
did, that the mistake of our time is in being
governed by the ignorant mass of opinion, instead of by thinkers and men who know something. How great that was of Gladstone,
" He has no foresight because he has no insight." Mr. Arnold never said a wiser thing,
and when he says that Gladstone will lead his
party (after describing what the party lacks)
by watching their minds and adapting his
programme and using his ease of speech to

gain the end — He *is* a party leader, and not a statesman. Does n't it seem as if it must fret a man like Arnold to the quick to go on saying things as he has and seeing people ignore them, then dispute them, then say that they were God's truth, when the whole thing has become a matter of history and it is too late to have them do the immediate good he hoped to effect?

Sunday night, *November*, 1884.

I am getting sleepy, for I must confess that it is past bedtime. I went to church this morning, but this afternoon I have been far afield, way over the hill and beyond, to an unusual distance. Alas, when I went to see my beloved big pitch-pine tree that I loved best of all the wild trees that lived in Berwick, I found only the broad stump of it beside the spring, and the top boughs of it scattered far and wide. It was a real affliction, and I thought *you* would be sorry, too, for such a mournful friend as sat down and counted the rings to see how many years old her tree was, and saw the broad rings when good wet summers had helped it grow and narrow ones when there had been a drought, and read as much of its long biography as she could. But

the day was very lovely, and I found many pleasures by the way and came home feeling much
refreshed. I found such a good little yellow
apple on one of the pasture trees, and I
laughed to think how you would be looking
at the next bite. It was *very* small, but I nib-
bled it like a squirrel. I found a white-weed
daisy fully blown, but only an inch high, so
that it looked as if somebody had snapped it
off and dropped it on the ground; and I was
in some underbrush, going along the slope,
and saw a crow come toward me flying low,
and when I stood still he did not see me and
came so close that I could hear his wings
creak their feathers — and nearly in the same
spot I thought I heard the last of the "creak-
its." I wished for you so much, it was a day
you would have loved.

Friday evening, SOUTH BERWICK [1885].

Today has been very hot and I have read
with great delight the book of Edwin Arnold's,
which I did n't send back after all, and I am
most glad to have it. More than that I want
you to read parts of it, for it is charmingly
done, so modest and manly and wise, and when
he gets to Ceylon all the Buddhists turn out

to do him honor. He has a grave conference
with an old priest, who thanks him for what
he has done for Buddhism, and then Arnold
asks him if there are any Mahatmas, to which
the priest answers no, none at all! If we had
better interpreters of Buddha's teaching we
might reach heights and depths of power and
goodness that are now impossible; but we
have fallen from the old wisdom and none of us
today are so advanced. There are all sorts of
interesting things in this "India Revisited";
one is that the Mayflower was chartered for
the East Indian trade after her Pilgrim experiences, and was sunk on her last voyage with
a cargo of rice!! I don't know why I found
that so *wildly* interesting!!

June, 1885.

Such a hot and agreeable day as yesterday
was! We played on the beach at Wells, but
not quite so hard as at York, the sun being
hotter. I got pretty tired, but enjoyed it all
vastly, and met with many old and fond friends
at the fish-houses,— R—— M——, and F——,
whom I wrote the story about, and old D——
B——, who can't go out fishing any more, so
that he sits at home and *knits stockings* and
thinks on his early days as an able seaman in

foreign parts. His wife died two or three years ago and he calls her " Poor dear! " when he talks about her. And there was big C. D. and big H. R., who pulled him out of the waves in an adverse squall at the Banks once, so that they are famous pals; all the old fishermen whom I have known since these many years; and A—— and L—— P—— and younger fry, who were also cordial and yet not *so* dear. I lagged along from one fish-house door to the next, and thought I was n't going to see D—— B——, the knitter, but early in the afternoon he rolled along as if he trod a quarter-deck all the way, and mentioned after a time that he saw me driving down — he saw a team and *got his glass* and found out it was I. My heart was quite touched when I found that he had n't been over to the moorings but once before this spring! I don't think from the looks of him that he will be missing "Poor dear" a great while longer. Yet he asked for some good books of stories, *detective ones,* none of your lovesick kind, which he could n't go! I must betake me to Wells again before long with a selection of literary offerings, G—— H——, the elder, being also a great reader, but of another stamp

and really one of the best-informed men I ever
knew, never forgetting anything apparently;
and when I tried to tell him about being at
St. Augustine, he told me the Indian names
at the Fort, and much else that had slipped
my mind. The drive home was as lovely as it
could be, the country so green and the farms
all so tidy, and the sheep and cattle thick in
the pastures, with such a sunset across all the
western sky.

This morning I have been to church, and
this afternoon I rested and read, chiefly the
"Alchemist," which is a great story, all the
early part of it. I think that Balzac got tired
of it toward the end — there where he makes
Margaret regain her lost fortune over and
over, as a lobster grows a new claw.

Thursday afternoon, 23 July, 1885.

Now comes the news of General Grant's
death, which is a relief in a way. I think nothing could be more pathetic than the records
of his last fight with his unvanquishable
enemy. No two men I have ever seen came
up to Grant and Tennyson in GREATNESS.
Tennyson first, I must say that. Good heavens, what a thing it is for a man of Grant's

deliberate, straightforward, comprehending mind, to sit day after day with that pain clutching at his throat, looking death straight in the face! and with all his clear sight he was no visionary or seer of spiritual things. It must have made him awfully conscious of all that lay this side the boundary. And now he knows all, the step is taken, and the mysterious moment of death proves to be a moment of waking. How one longs to take it for one's self!

Thursday evening, 1886.

This table is so overspread with the story of the Normans that I can hardly find room to put my paper down on it. I started in for work this afternoon, having been on the strike long enough, as one might say; but I only did a little writing, for I found that I must read the whole thing through, I have forgotten so much of it.

Do read Miss Preston's paper about Pliny the younger in the "Atlantic." It is full of charming things, and as readable as possible. It sent me to my old favorite, the elder Pliny's "Natural History," but I could n't find it in any of the book-cases downstairs, and I was too lazy to go up for it. Oh, you should see the old

robin by my bed-room window a-fetching up
her young family! I long to have you here
to watch the proceedings. She is a slack house-
keeper, is that robin, for the blown-away ruffles
that she wove into her nest have suffered so
much from neglect, combined with wind and
weather, that they ravel out in unsightly
strings. But oh, the wide mouths of the three
young ones, — how they do reach up and
gape altogether when she comes near the nest
with a worm! How can she attend to the mu-
ral decorations of her home? I am getting to
be very intimate with the growing family. I
hate every pussy when I think what a paw
might do. I waited by the window an hour
at tea-time, spying them.

I have finished "Pendennis" with deep
regret, for I have enjoyed it enormously. It
is truly a great story, more simple and sin-
cere and inevitable than "Vanity Fair." It
seems as much greater than Tolstoi's "Anna
Karenina" as it is more full of true humanity.
It belongs to a more developed civilization, to
a far larger interpretation of Christianity. But
people are not contented at reading "Pendennis" every few years and with finding it always new as they grow more able to under-

stand it. Thackeray is so great, a great Christian. He does not affect, he humbly learns and reverently tries to teach out of his own experience. " Pendennis " belongs to America just now more than it belongs to England, but we must forget it and go and read our Russian. Yes, he has a message too, but most people understand it so little that he amuses them and excites their wonder like Jules Verne.

I am writing before breakfast. I have finished " Hugh Wynne" and loved it, with its fresh air and manliness, and — to me — exquisite charm. Don't you know what Tennyson said: " I love those large, still books ! "

Monday morning.

Little old Miss Elizabeth C. is dead at ninety-two, after a miserable year or two when all of her has been dead but her small body. I went down to see her nephew, and found him as bereaved as possible. I don't go into the old house very often, but yesterday I was so moved by the sight of certain things, and especially of an ottoman on which I used to sit very high in the air and perilous, both with a sense of the occasion, and being off sound-

ings as to the floor. Such pound-cakes as I
have eaten on that ottoman! Somehow all the
hospitality of those days came back in touching contrast to the empty, womanless rooms
yesterday. Miss C. has always been a recluse.
I have seldom seen her on the street and
but a few times at church. She would have
been a nun in early days. The bustling world
was always too much for her. Dear, kindly
soul that she was, with a pair of beautiful child-
like blue eyes, which seemed forever young,
though I can't remember when her thin bent
little figure did n't look old. She always hid
away from the gayeties of the house. Her
mother was a kind of little old duchess with
great social faculty, a friend of Lafayette in
the war times, so that on his royal progress he
took pains to come to see her. I used to hear
the call related with great particularity when
I was a little girl. These were Boston Cush-
ings originally, and were for a long time new-
comers, having moved to Berwick in 1795,
when Berwick, though small, was as proper a
place to live in as Boston, " at least so thinks "
Madam Cushing. I must not forget to tell you
that Miss Elizabeth said a year or two ago,
when that base-looking Methodist Church was

building near by, "Charles, is that a ship
I see? when are they going to launch?" It
was a curious memory of her childish visits at
the old Wallingford house, her grandfather's,
which stood across the river from the Hamilton house, when ships were built there and
the river, so quiet now, was a busy place. Too
much of Miss Elizabeth, says a patient friend,
but I am always delighting in reading the old
Berwick, picturesque as it was, under the
cover of the new life which seems to you so
dull and unrewarding in most ways. "Where
every prospect pleases," etc., ought to be your
hymn for Berwick, the which I don't suggest
unmercifully, but rather compassionately, and
with a plaintive feeling at heart.

I don't know when I have had such a delightful day of reading as I had yesterday.
Parts of Rousseau's "Confessions" were perfectly enchanting, — the bits about his walks;
and whatever he writes about, he is never dis-
gusting to me, as many of his age are. I
never began to know the "Confessions" before. It was my *first time*, as Mrs. Bell says.
I also read a good bit in Daniel's poems, and
was so snug and lazy by a big fire in the fireplace. John suggests the furnace, being evi-

dently tired of getting in enough big walnut logs for all the fireplaces every morning; but I beg off selfishly. The house never seems half so pleasant when the fireplaces are cold. Give my dear love to Marigold [1] when you see her.

Tuesday evening.

I need not tell you what a joyful home-coming it was. Mother's look as she came running out to meet Mary was something that I never shall forget. It was like some old painter's picture of a Bible scene! With her arms out, and her aging face and figure. And such a time all the afternoon, and the un-packing and presents galore, and charming photographs as thick as the fallen leaves with-out. I kept wishing for you to "be to it," Pinny with such splendour! Burne-Jones' photographs, new ones, and *big!* and a seal-skin cape to her shoulders, and an Edinburgh pin, and a new ivory brush (needed!), and a *beautiful* piece of best lace, and some new un-dergarments, and stockings, and a best white petticoat, and Oh *such* a lot of things! I ought to be Sandpiper to properly enumerate and describe!

[1] Mrs. James Lodge.

Wednesday night.

I have had a lovely day. I felt tired and flustered with things to do, so I took John and two horses and skipped to "York Long Sands," and feel the better for it. The road was muddy after the rain, and the country was so green and fresh. I was really anxious to see dear old Miss Barrell, having heard that she was very feeble. When I arrived, the house was orderly and *so* lonesome, and the good woman who takes care of the poor soul told me that she had not been sleeping for night after night, that her mind was gone and she could hardly speak. She asked if I would go up, and I said yes. There was the sunshiny great bedroom, looking out on the river, and the most minute, attenuated figure of my poor old friend in her great chair with her dinner, — such a careful, good dinner! — spread before her, and she seemed to be playing with it without eating, like a child. I went close to her and spoke to her, sad at heart with the change I saw, for she has evidently had a stroke which has dulled one side of her face. Then such a lovely flash of recognition! She took hold of me with her poor old bird's claw of a hand and kissed and kissed me and tried

to talk; her eyes were full of life and of love,
as if I had found her in the prison of her body
and would understand. She tried to say things
and really did manage a few short sentences,
and I guessed at others, but alas I had to miss
the rest; but the thought was all there, and
she was so full of pleasure at seeing me, having me come to see her in prison, for I can
think of it in no other way. Dear quaint little
creature, nobody knows how appealing it was.
You see I have to write you all about it. I
dare say she does n't always know people, and
that often her mind *is* gone, but she did know
me and I knew her, and I hated to take myself away from her at last. She always asked
for Mother in the old days, and that was one
of the things she said clearest today. All her
touching little politenesses and acts of hospitality were evidently in her mind, but it was
like listening to an indistinct telephone. I
caught one flash of her old manner when I
happened to speak of a family she disapproved.
" Pack o' fools," she whispered, and we did
have such a laugh, the last of all our laughs
together, I fear me. It was dreadful when she
said things that I could n't make out, but I
took refuge in telling her everything I could

think of, that she might like to hear, speaking
slowly and clearly, and she almost always knew
and tried to answer. Nothing was really alive
but her eyes, like Heine's. I think she has had
some new things to think of, in her prison.
The good nurse hardly knew what to make of
us, but she is very kind and capable. I dare
say this was a sudden flicker of her old self,
but was n't it wonderful? Perhaps the shadow
fell on her mind again directly, and she has
been in the pitiful state they described ; but
you can't think how I rejoice to think I went
to see her.

October.

The two notes you sent me tonight are
very dear prints of your footsteps along the
path of life. A sentimental Pinny to express
herself so, but she feels it to the bottom of
her heart. Miss Grant [1] is in the full tide of
successful narration. She described an acquaintance this morning as a "meek-looking
woman, but *very* understanding!" I have
not been writing today. I should have been
called off at any rate a good deal, so I did
some hammering and housekeeping this morning, and "box-pleated" sixteen breadths of

[1] The village dressmaker.

silk ruffle this afternoon. (I think we shall have the little lace frock. It is not going to be a great deal of work, and is getting on capitally.)

Sunday afternoon, *December*, 1888.

I have just been reading Mr. Arnold's essay on George Sand, and finished it with tears in my eyes. How beautiful, and how full of inspiration it is! We cannot be grateful enough to either of them, and yet how little I really know her books! I am willing to study French very hard all winter in order to read her comfortably in the spring!

This morning at church I was dreadfully bored with a sermon, and I made up a first-rate story which will have to be written very soon after Christmas. I must tell you all about it. How soon we shall be talking now, if all goes well, and good-bye to letters for a while. Tomorrow I shall be busy getting my things together, and doing up Christmas bundles. I am not sure whether I shall take the half past ten train or the half past two, so go your ways, dear, and I hope you will find me there when you come home to dinner.

That story of Tolstoi's was such an excitement that I did not sleep until almost morn-

ing. What a wonderful thing it is! I long to
talk with you about it, but do let us think a
good deal. It startled me because I was dimly
feeling the same kind of motive (not the same
plan) in writing the " Gray Man." Nobody
cared much for it, but it is the same sort of
story, it is there. I wish that you would look
it over and see. I believed in that story so
that I would have published it if I had to
make the type. If I can only feel that I am in
the right road, in one sense nothing else matters. I have felt something of what Tolstoi
has been doing all the way along. I can tell
you half a dozen stories where I tried to say
it, " Lady Terry," " Beyond the Toll-gate "
and this " Gray Man." Now and then it came
clearer to me. I never felt the soul of Tolstoi's
work until last night, something of it in Katia,
but now I know what he means, and I know that
I can dare to keep at the work I sometimes
have despaired about because you see people
are always caught by fringes of it and liked
the stories if they liked them at all for some
secondary quality. I know there is something
true, and yet I myself have often looked only
at the accidental and temporary part of
them.

Another postcard from Mr. Freeman.[1] He has found about Maurice!! and is more friendly than ever. How can I live up to this correspondence? I am going to head him off and keep him quiet for a while by telling him that I have only a few of my books at hand.

Friday night.

I have read most of the nice letters and enjoyed them so much while I sat by the light, talking and listening by turns. Now I have stolen into the office for a word. Here is Eldress Harriet, who has given up the things of this world and can say stoutly at her letter's end that they can "hold on fast by God," as the old version of the Psalms has it, through their Shaker faith! And dear Mrs. Stowe, with her new suggestion for my happiness, standing ready like a switchman at the division by the rails. How sweet her letters are, though, — hers to you most lovely, for it says all we felt, and knew she thought that evening.

[March, 1889.]

Now this is a hopeful sign. I just looked out of the window and some boys have found

[1] The historian.

a dry spot on the sidewalk and are playing marbles. The mud is still very deep and the snow-drifts very high, but the hills are like big leopards and tigers ready for a pounce at something, with their brown and white spots. I never was more glad to see the brown spots show themselves, and shouldn't you think the grass would be glad to have the snow go off, so that the sun can shine on it and the wind blow it? Once I should have been in a hurry to go racing off for hepaticas, but it is too early at any rate, and I say to myself that I never did care very much for those flowers, and I find I am growing old and lazy and can let them bloom and wilt again without any sorrow. Hepaticas are like some people, very dismal blue, with cold hands and faces. I had to stop to think about wild flowers, and I believe there is nothing dearer than a trig little company of anemones in a pasture, all growing close together as if they kept each other warm, and wanted the whole sun to themselves, beside. They had no business to wear their summer frocks so early in the year.

I am bewitched with a story, though I have nothing to say to you about it yet.

Sunday evening, 1889.

I have been reading "Pendennis" with *such* pleasure. What a beautiful story! I long to read some pages to you, for the humanity — the knowledge of life and the sympathy with every-day troubles is more and more wonderful. It all seems new to me, and to follow Thackeray through the very days when he was at work upon it, as we can in the Scribner letters, is such a joy. I got "Law Lane" in proof yesterday in excellent season for the Christmas number, one would think. Mr. Burlingame hoped that I could shorten it a little, and I have been working over it. He has great plans for his Christmas number and there are many things to go in. He seems pleased with "Law Lane," so is its humble author, but you are not to tell. I have not been out today, except to the garden to pick myself a luncheon of currants.

Later.

I am almost through "Pendennis." I do wish you would read it pretty soon! perhaps next winter!! And a story which has been lagging a good while is beginning to write itself. Its name is "A Player Queen," and it hopes to be liked. Miss Preston's article looks

very interesting in the "Atlantic," about the
Russian novels, but I have not found the
right half hour to read it. Oh, my dear, it is
such a comfort to think of you in the dear
house, with the sea calling and all the song
sparrows singing by turns to try and make
you sing, too.

I was much moved by your news about
poor Mr. R——. I am glad that the old man is
likely to be released, but *there* is a little round
world of two people going to fall to pieces.
All the better for them in some ways, too, but
with all their provoking narrowness there is
something very appealing in their relation to
each other, and she is going to find life very
hard alone, simply because it has been so narrow, and she has no great outlook or prepara-
tion for unselfish usefulness. I dare say you
are going to be able to help her by and by,
but now all that anybody can do for her is to
try to make her feel that there are a few kind
hearts that are truly sorry for her.

Friday night, 1889.

I thought of you today, for I was over in
the fields and found a brookful of delicious
crisp water-cresses, but I shall let them grow

until you come, for I don't think anybody
cares much for them. I pulled two or three
and washed them in the brook and thought
there never were any so good. Some day we
will take a piece of bread and butter and go
there and have a banquet.

There is a book I wish you would take to
Manchester for me, or is it there already?
The life of Fox and somebody else. Since I
read the Warren Hastings essay I have been
wishing to pick up more about that time, and
about Burke and Sheridan.

Last night I had a perfect delight re-
reading Dorothy Wordsworth's Tour in Scotland. I finished it by hurrying a little at the
end, but there is no more charming book in
the world. It is just our book, and the way
we enjoy things is n't it, when we are footing
it out of doors?

I was delighted to find so many birds today, golden robins, blackbirds, bobolinks, and
only Sandpiper knows what else. It was
beautiful in the fields, and so resting.

Saturday morning, 1889.

I am waiting for your letter to come, and it
seems a long half hour. A thriftless person

when there are so many things to do, but somehow I did not get to sleep last night, except
for two or three naps which were rather too un-
easy for comfort. I had one most beautiful
time which was after your own heart. It began to be light, and after spending some time
half out of the window hearing one bird tune
up after another, I half dressed myself and
went out and stayed until it was bright day-
light. I went up the street, and out into the
garden, where I had a beautiful time, and was
neighborly with the hop-toads and with a joyful robin who was sitting on a corner of the
barn, and I became very intimate with a big
poppy which had made every arrangement to
bloom as soon as the sun came up. There was
a bright little waning moon over the hill,
where I had a great mind to go, but there
seemed to be difficulties, as I might be missed,
or somebody might break into the house
where I had broken out. Were n't you awake,
too, very early? I thought so, and I was
equally certain that other people were asleep.
Really, so much happened in that hour that
I could make a book of it — I had a great
temptation to go to writing.

I have done so many things today that I

should like to write them down and see what
they were. There was a piece gone off the
top of the three gilded feathers on the breakfast room looking-glass, so I carved a feather
top out of pine wood and stuck it on and
gilded it most satisfactorily, and then I set
Stubby and an impoverished friend who
needed money for the Fourth to digging plan-
tains out of the grass at fifteen cents the
hundred, whereupon they doubled their dili-
gence until they got $1.65 out of me at din-
ner time!! And I transplanted a lot of little
sunflowers and put hellebore on the gooseberry
bushes and wrote a lot of notes for the " Berwick Scholar " on account of the Centennial
arrangements, and went down street twice and
— but I won't tell you, yes, I will — the
little Beverly doggie came by express! and is
ardently beloved by Stubs, and that took
time, and after dinner I went to Beaver Dam
with John about a carriage painter and another
errand, and then I dressed me all up and went
and made two elegant calls, and then I came
home and wrote this.

Sunday, 5th July.

. . . I have been reading the beginning
of " The Pearl of Orr's Island " and finding

it just as clear and perfectly original and
strong as it seemed to me in my thirteenth or
fourteenth year, when I read it first. I never
shall forget the exquisite flavor and reality of
delight that it gave me. I do so long to read
it with you. It is classical — historical —
anything you like to say, if you can give it
high praise enough. I have n't read it for ten
years at least, but *there it is!* Alas, that she
could n't finish it in the same noble key of
simplicity and harmony ; but a poor writer is
at the mercy of much unconscious opposition.
You must throw everything and everybody
aside at times, but a woman made like Mrs.
Stowe cannot bring herself to that cold self-
ishness of the moment for one's work's sake,
and the recompense for her loss is a divine
touch here and there in an incomplete piece of
work. I felt at the funeral that none of us
could really know and feel the greatness of
the moment, but it has seemed to grow more
great to me ever since. I love to think of the
purple flowers you laid on the coffin.

I hope the York visit will be worth while. I
look forward to seeing Mrs. Lawrence more than
anything, and to the funny Indians, and the
lights across the harbor at night. I am so glad

you have seen the little place and know where
I shall be.

Thursday night, 4 *December*, 1889.

Such a day ! — the weather could not be
resisted, and I went to York — you would
have truly loved it, for I never knew more
delicious weather, as bright and sweet as Indian summer, only more bracing. I had my
luncheon out of doors and sat afterward in an
old boat on the pebbles and watched the great
waves of a high tide. I could not bear to
come away. You never saw anything more
beautiful than that great stretch of shore, and
the misty sea, and the gulls, so lonely, so full,
and so *friendly*, somehow. I went chiefly for
the sake of seeing my old friend, and found
her in a mood that matched the day, all her
wildness and strangeness of last summer quite
gone, and a sweet pathos and remembrance
come in their stead. She was so glad to see
me, that my heart cries to think of her. —
She said once, "I want you to thank your
mother for bringing you into the world, you
have been such a pleasure to me." — And
then I must go to her closets and find her best
cap, and a new double gown, and a better
shoulder-shawl, and help her put them on be-

cause I had come! She has grown so thin and small, as if she were slowly turning into a fairy, and it was so sweet to see her less troubled, though she remembered perfectly the last time I was there, broken as she seemed to me then. The sunshine filled the quaint old room and we had a delightful long talk, though once in a while she would be a little bewildered, and tell me over and over again about her sister's death. " I lay down beside her," she would say, " and I thought she seemed very cold, but I put my arms round her " ; and then she would cry, and I would talk about something else, until in a minute or two she would be smiling again through her sad old tears. As long as I could see the house, she was standing at her chamber window and waving her handkerchief to me, and I promised to go down again the first time I came home. She seems very feeble. I had a strong feeling that I should not see her again. I must tell you that she said with strange emphasis, " I have seen Betsey, she came one night and stood beside my bed; it shocked me a good deal, but I saw her, and one of my brothers came with her." As she told me this I believed it was the truth, and no delusion of her unsteady brain. I ought not to write any more, but somehow there is a great deal to tell you.

This morning I was out, taking a drive about town with John and I saw *such* a coast from way up the long hillside down to the tavern garden, and directly afterward down in the village I beheld Stubby faring along with his sled, which is about as large as a postage-stamp. So I *borryed* it, as you say, and was driven up to the top of the hill street and down I slid over that pound-cake frosting of a coast most splendid, and meekly went back to the village and returned the sled. Then an hour later in bursts Stubby, with shining morning face: " There were two fellows that said Aunt Sarah was the boss, she went down side-saddle over the hill *just like the rest of the boys!* "

I have been reading Christopher North's " Genius and Character of Burns " — father's old Wiley and Putnam copy — with such delight, and this evening I got down the poems and longed to have them with you. We don't read Burns half enough, do we ? And when I read again the eloquence of the Wilson book, I wondered at that dull placidity that was lately printed in the "Atlantic," yet I was most grateful to it for freshening my thought of the big Scotsman. Do let us read bits of the Burns together some time, just for the bigness of his affection and praise.

I wrote until after dark this afternoon, and then went out to walk in the early moonlight, down the street by the Academy, and even up on the hill back of the Academy itself. There was a great grey cloud in the west, but all the rest of the sky was clear, and it was very beautiful. When one goes out of doors and wanders about alone at such a time, how wonderfully one becomes part of nature, like an atom of quick-silver against a great mass. I hardly keep my separate consciousness, but go on and on until the mood has spent itself.

Madame Sand's mother is astray out of a Dickens book, but I don't know which one. I wish I knew that kind of people well enough to write about them ; they are dreadfully interesting sometimes. Today I am plunged into the depths of the rural districts, and this promised to be one of my dear country stories like the "Only Son." Good heavens! what a wonderful kind of chemistry it is that evolves all the details of a story and writes them presently in one flash of time! For two weeks I have been noticing a certain string of things and having hints of character, etc., and day before yesterday the plan of the story comes into my mind, and in half an hour I have put all the little words and ways into their places and can read it off to myself like print. Who does it? for I grow more and more sure that I don't!

I am going to grapple with the difficulty of a run-away husband. I wish I could tell you all about it, but I mean to have it done in two or three days. I ought to be preparing the " Dulham Ladies" and "A Gray Man " for " the press," but it is better to get hold of this new one while I can. I send you a " Century." Do read the Virginia girl's paper about the war. We have often heard bits of talk that match it, but those pathetic days have never been more truthfully and delicately written down.

Saturday.

I had a perfectly delightful evening from old Dr. Lord last night. I wished for you. He really is so interesting now. He was talking about his English experiences at the time he lived there three or four years and married his wife. He knew Cardinal Wiseman and Archbishop Whately, and Carlyle, about whom he talked enchantingly. It made me feel as if I had gone to the door in Cheyne Row and had "Mrs. Carlyle herself" come to open it, "a beautiful woman with delightful manners," and Carlyle come scolding downstairs (though he had made the appointment himself) and grumbling that Americans were all bores and he liked the Russians, a sober, thinking and acting people, and then he would grow very good-natured, and after a while take his company for a long walk;—cross old Dean Gaisford also appeared with that group of Oxford men. You could have drawn out much more, but indeed it was very interesting to me. Egotism is the best of a man after eighty. He is chiefly valuable then for what he has been, and for the wealth of his personality, and what is silly self-admiration at forty is a treasure of remembrance. The stand-point has changed.

I must say good-bye, but what savings we shall be telling over pretty soon. Don't forget things.

Wednesday evening
(with a great rain on the roof of the study).

I have been reading Mr. Arnold's " Essays
on Celtic Poetry " with perfect reverence for
him and his patience and wisdom. How much
we love him and believe in him, don't we?
Do you know this book and the essay on
translating Homer? I long to read it all with
you.

Sunday evening, *Autumn*.

I hope that you have had a good day. I
have been to church myself for a wonder,
since from one reason or another I have not
been preached at for some months! This afternoon, after the communion service, I had a
great pleasure in seeing the very old church
silver which is not often used, and some time
I wish to show it to you. One exquisite old
flagon is marked 1674, and the cups are such
beautiful shapes. They keep it packed away
in the bank, — very properly, — and usually
use a new set bought thirty or forty years ago.
I dare say that some of the old came from
England, — it is really so interesting with all
the givers' names and inscriptions put on in
such quaint pretty lettering.

Yes, it is quite magnificent about the copy-

right bill, and I like to have my country
honest at last about the Spoliation Claims. I
told Mother yesterday that she must buy a
piece of plate and have it marked French
Spoliation Claims, 1891, and have it handed
down.

You never saw such a lot of snow in your
towny life as is now piled up in this single
hamlet. It is really a huge lot, and so drifted
and tumbled about, and every little while today the northwest wind would blow, and the
air would be full for awhile. Jocky seems to
think it is a very hard winter.

Mr. Putnam has just got back from London, and I find that I shall probably begin
my proofs[1] within a fortnight. I am forgetting the worrisome detail a little now, and
dread taking it up again, but perhaps they
will hurry through and shorten my miseries.
" Vanity Fair" is read through, a very great
book, and for its time Tolstoi and Zola and
Daudet and Howells and Mark Twain and
Turgenieff and Miss Thackeray of *this* day
all rolled into one, so wise and great it is and
reproachful and realistic and full of splendid
scorn for meanness and wickedness, which

[1] The story of the Normans.

scorn the Zola school seems to lack. And the
tenderness and sweetness of the book is heavenly, that is all I can say about it. I am
brimful of things to say.

Monday.

The big ash tree in front of the house is so
nearly dead that it must come down, and the
big elm between here and Carrie's, the dearest tree of my childhood and all my days, is
all hollow and all the weight of it is toward
the house, so that after much consultation we
are afraid to let it stand through the winter,
and that must be chopped down, too. I shall
be glad when they are done and cleared
away. I dread it so much that it quite haunts
me, but I was shocked to find the other day in
what a dangerous state the old tree was. It
wouldn't be pleasant to have it prod through
the roof; in fact, I begin to feel as if it were
holding itself up just as long as it could, in
a kind of misery of apprehension, poor old
tree! It seems as if it must know all about
us. Then one of the spruces is also to be
slain to let in more light; that will meet
your approval. . . . Today I have been reading, for one thing, Mrs. Oliphant's "Royal
Edinburgh," a most delightful book, — partic-

ularly the chapter about Mary Queen of Scots
and John Knox, and the last chapter about
Sir Walter, which we really must read together some time. It is a *beautiful* piece of
work.

You will be much amused to hear that the
funny old man in the linen duster whom I
caught sight of at Chapel Station has really
been the making of the "Atlantic" sketch. I
mean to begin him this morning and get well
on with him before the girls come. His name
proves to be Mr. Teaby, and he is one of those
persons who peddle essences and perfumery and
a household remedy or two, and foot it about
the country with limp enameled cloth bags.
What do you think of Mr. Teaby now?
Teaby is the name, and he talks with sister
Pinkham about personal and civic matters on
a depot platform in the rural districts. Don't
you think an editor would feel encouraged?

Tuesday evening.

DEAR, — Oh, I did have such a good time
today! I went to see some huge pine trees
down in the edge of Wells, — an out-of-the-
way road, but I always knew that these pines
were the biggest in the state and had a great

desire to see them. Oh, do go next summer
to see the most superb creatures that ever
grew! I don't believe that their like is in
New England. More than four feet through
their great trunks, and standing so tall that
their great green tops seem to belong to the
next world. In all my life I never was in such
glorious woods. I long to take you there.
Afterward I went into the farmhouse and had
a perfectly beautiful time. I knew they were
old patients of father's, and that he used to
like to go there, but I was not prepared to
find Doris and Dan Lester a dozen years older
than when we met them last!!! And they
had read works of Pinny and were so affectionate and delightful and talked about father
— and made a little feast for she, and it was
a perfectly beautiful good time.

(TO T. B. ALDRICH)

SOUTH BERWICK, MAINE.

MY DEAR FRIEND, — I am much pleased
at hearing of your collegiate honors, and especially (from some one who was present) of the
delightful and hearty applause. How I should
have clapped my hands and pounded if I had

been there !! Did the boys use to pound
their feet on the floor in Portsmouth? Only
a very great moment on the stage of the
village hall wins such expression here. Anything that does you and your lovely work
honor wakes something very good and un-
speakable in my heart. I should have seen the
author of a poem called "Elmwood," and a
story called "A Bad Boy," and other poems and
other stories, too many to count here, stand
up in the Sanders Theatre, and I should have
been so glad to think he and I were friends.

I hope that there may be a little better
news from your two old invalids — that these
are days of less pain and discomfort. I think
so often of you and Lilian waiting and watching there. I am glad you are out in the
country and not in town. With love to you
both.

(TO MRS. FIELDS)

HOME, Saturday afternoon.

Mr. Howells thinks that this age frowns
upon the romantic, that it is no use to write
romance any more ; but dear me, how much
of it there is left in every-day life after all.
It must be the fault of the writers that such

writing is dull, but what shall I do with my
"White Heron" now she is written? She
is n't a very good magazine story, but I love
her, and I mean to keep her for the beginning
of my next book and the reason for Mrs.
Whitman's pretty cover. In the meantime I
will simply state that the next story is called
"Marsh Rosemary," and I made it up as I
drove to the station in Wells this morning. It
deals with real life. Somehow dear, dull old
Wells is a first-rate place to find stories in.
Do you remember how we drove up that long
straight road across the marshes last summer?
It was along there the Marsh Rosemary grew.

I have been reading an old copy of Donne's
poems with perfect delight. They seem new
to me just now, even the things I knew best.
We must read many of them together. I
must have my old copy mended; it is quite
shabby, with its label lost and leaves working
out from the binding.

Thursday morning, Decoration Day.

There is going to be an unwonted parade
in honor of the day and I am glad; for usually
everybody trots off to Dover or Portsmouth,

and nothing is done here except to put the pathetic little flags about the burying-grounds. It seems to me that I have just begun to understand how grown people felt about the war in the time of it, — at any rate it brought tears to my eyes yesterday when John said that over two hundred men went from this little town to the war. You can see how many young sons of old farmers, and how many men out of their little shops, and people who had nobody to leave in their places, went to make up that number. Yesterday I went traveling in my own land, and found the most exquisite place that ever was. We followed a woods road into an old farm where I used to go with father years and years ago (the first time I ever knew anemones, was there, I remember). It is high on a great rocky hillside and deep in the woods, and what I had completely forgotten was the most exquisite of glens. I am not going to try and describe it except to say that I never have seen a more exquisite spot, and I must certainly take you to see it. It is so far off the road that it might be in the depths of the White Mountains as to loneliness, and it is much less often visited. I remember it vaguely, as a little child, when

I saw it often, but I had completely forgotten it.

I did have the most beautiful time yesterday afternoon. I feel as if I had seen another country in Europe. Oh, a great deal better than that, though I only went wandering over a great tract of pasture-land down along the river. You would think it is such a lovely place, and I shall have to write about it one of these days, for I saw so many things. I never had known anything beyond the edges of it before. It was the sweetest weather in the world, and Roger went. But last night there was a dismal time, for the bad bowwows got into the parlor together, and first thing I knew there was a pitched battle, and I was afraid the lamps and everything would be tipped over before I could get hold of anybody's collar, and Roger passed a suffering night with a lame paw and broke my rest all to pieces with his whining, and Browny's ear was damaged, and dogs are at a discount.

Wednesday evening.

Sometimes, the business part of writing grows very noxious to me, and I wonder if in heaven our best thoughts — poet's thoughts, especially — will not be flowers, somehow, or some sort of beautiful live things that stand about and grow, and don't have to be chaffered over and bought and sold. It seems as bad as selling our fellow beings, but being in this world everything must have a body, and a material part, so covers and leaves and publishing generally come under that head, and is another thing to make us wish to fly away and be at rest!

[One day these verses came with the usual bulletin of prose.]

Right here, where noisiest, narrowest is the street;
Where gaudy shops bedeck the crowded way;
Where idle newsboys in vindictive play
Dart to and fro with venturesome bare feet;
Here, where the bulletins from fort and fleet
Tell gaping readers what's amiss today,
Where sin bedizens, folly makes too gay,
And all are victims of their own conceit;
With these ephemeral insects of an hour
That war and flutter, as they downward float
In some pale sunbeam that the spring has brought,
Where this vain world is revelling in power;
I met great Emerson, serene, remote,
Like one adventuring on seas of thought.

Wednesday morning.

I wrote hard and fast yesterday morning,
and in the afternoon, we all went to drive,
and had the most delightful expedition to an
old farm up in the wild country between here
and the sea, where the rough woods come close
to painfully cleared little green fields and pastures. Don't you remember my telling you about
a charming waterfall? Well, it was there again
that I went, but furthermore, to see a great
view from the top of the high hill beyond.
Then we took a wide sweep round into another
road and so home, as Mr. Pepys says. I must
tell you about that farmhouse at the old place,
near the brook and fen. It stands very high,
but has no view of the country, in summer at
least, and a mile and a half from the main
road.

We went in to see old Mr. G., who has
been long ill and for a year bedridden, but
was sitting up at last yesterday, looking down
the lane up which so few people are likely
to come; but it seemed a great pleasure because we ensued! and he absolutely cried
when he saw mother! He is a good old fellow,
who in old days brought the best of walnut

wood and other farm-stores, and like all his
kind, considered father and mother to be final!
He has left, out of a large household, only one
son and two orphan grand-children, and there
they live in that solitary place. The house is
bare and clean and looks as if men kept it,
though just as we were coming away a little
girl came out of a wood-path, home from
school, in a pink dress, like a shy flower. She
will soon grow. Listen to this, dear: the man's
wife sat in that same bare room looking down
the lane, thirty years, and for twenty-five she
could not feed herself, a martyr to the worst
sort of rheumatism and everything else. One
of the best souls in the world. It makes my
heart ache to think of her and of all the rest
of them; generations have lived there, and most
of them die young. There is a swamp back
of the house out of which the beauty of the
waterfall comes like a mockery of all the pain
and trouble, as if it were always laughing.
But those people could hardly be persuaded
to put their house in another spot; when the
old one wore out thirty years ago or more,
they built another on its cellar. There was a
white rose-bush within reach of the old man's
hand. Indeed, I call that region the White Rose

Road, for every farmhouse has a tall bush by its front door, and yesterday they were in full bloom. I did n't mean to write such a long chapter when I began, and I must fly to my work.

Don't you think it would be nice for us to have the " Revue " [1] again this summer just for a few months ? I have a feeling that I should like it, — and as if I wished to get as near to France as possible, without going there. I have a curious sense of delight in the fragrance that blows out of Madame Blanc's letter every time I take it out of its envelope, it is so refined, so personal, and of the past.

I have the greatest joy in reading Wordsworth lately. I can't get enough of him, and I take snatches of time for " The Leech-Gatherer," and the other short ones, and feel as if I had lived a week in going through each one of them.

Thursday morning.

I mourn for poor Crabby — poor little dog ! I hate to think we shall never see him again. I never liked him so much as I have this summer,

[1] The *Revue des Deux Mondes.*

in his amiable and patient age. However, I had worried much about what should come next when he was blinder and feebler, and it is good to think that his days are done so comfortably. I am sure all the girls felt sorry as we do.

It is a grey day and looks like a cold rain, but John and Theodore, like "Benjy" and "Tom Brown," have gone to the Rochester fair, with smiles on their faces that seemed to tie behind and be quite visible as they walked away!

I have been reading "Miss Angel." It is a most lovely historical story. If you have n't got it, I want to send my little Tauchnitz one. Venice is so exquisitely drawn in it, and afterward in London, all the life of that day. Dr. Johnson comes along the street as if one's own eyes saw him. I think you have got "Miss Angel," but perhaps you can't put a hand on it.

I took down the two Choate volumes[1] yesterday, and read with unforgettable delight, — not that it was new altogether, but somehow new *then*.

[1] The biography of Rufus Choate.

May.

This is something I remember at this moment in Voltaire. " He labored at every new work as if he had his reputation still to make! " But oh, his letters! such grace, such " gaieté de cœur "! They are really wonderful, are they not? I only wish that there were more of them, and when I saw an edition of his works for sale in Libbie's catalogue, I was tempted to bid. I don't dare propose to Mother the bringing in of seventy volumes at one fell swoop! or it might be ninety-seven in the best edition.

Good morning, dear. I begin to set my day and to wonder if I can't spend a week from this coming Sunday with you. . . .

I hope you can get off to Manchester by the fourth or fifth, as you planned, for I can only get a few days there at first, for I find that the County Conference, dear to my heart, is coming on the eleventh, all the country ministers and their wives and delightful delegates who never appear to go anywhere else — nice old country women.

(to mr. and mrs. t. b. aldrich)

South Berwick, Maine, 23 *July*, 1890.

My dear Friends, — I began a letter to you the very week you went away, but I did not finish it, for my mother has been most dangerously ill, and only just now begins to seem as if she were getting well again. We have felt very anxious all these long weeks. I really am in a great hurry now to know where you are and what you have been doing. I was so overwhelmed when I got word of the change in the "Atlantic's" fortunes that I don't feel free to express myself even yet! But this I can say, that I am most grateful for and unforgetful of all the patience and kindness which my dear friend the editor has given me in these years that are past. One day I saw in the "Nation" that "one has learned to look for Miss Jewett's best work in the pages of the 'Atlantic'"; but I could read something deeper still between those lines and gladly owned to myself that it was due to many suggestions and much helpfulness that my sketches have a great deal of their (possible) value. I have been taught. so many lessons and been kept toward a better direction than

I could have found for myself. If I were not looking eagerly for your new work, dear Mr. T. B. A., and were not thankful that your time was your own now for your work's sake, I should lament more loudly than I do over the magazine's loss.

I wonder if you will go to Paris, and if you will see Madame Blanc? I had a delightful letter from her not long ago, written in the South of France, and sounding like one of George Sand's — say from the second volume of her Correspondence! She sent me a volume of S. O. J. all in French, which caused such pride of heart that no further remarks are ventured upon the subject!

(TO MRS. FIELDS)

Tuesday morning.

It seems as if two leaves for one had suddenly come out on the trees. Yesterday afternoon I went to the funeral of an old patient of my father on one of the old farms —where the neighbourhood minister preached and the old farmhouse was crowded with people — and then we all walked out, two by two, across a broad green field, with old-fashioned pall-bearers carrying the coffin by hand and

changing, — first four would take it, and then
four others who went before, just as it must
have been in England two hundred years ago.
There was such a long procession, a hundred
and thirty or forty, and all in little flocks, —
the father and mother and their big and little
children, by twos, following them, and then
another father and mother and their children.
Somehow it looked quite scriptural! and the
burying-ground was a little square out in the
middle of this great field, with tall high-standing
trees shading it. The whole scene was most
touching and simple and curiously *archaic*.
Usually the farming people have the hearse
come and do all the things that village people do.

I have been reading a really wonderful little
book by poor Richard Jefferies. I had never
even heard of it — " The Story of My Heart,"
he calls it, but it is really the expression of his
religious growth and aspiration toward higher
things. He finds little in conventional, or rather
formulated religions, but everything in an
eager belief in higher forms of life and unre-
vealed wisdom. He comes closer to these in
out - of - door life, as one might expect who
knows his other books, but his ability to put

into words the consciousness of life and individuality and relationship to eternity is something amazing. I have never known anything just like it. I thought of "thy friend"[1] as I read it, and of "Phantastes," which I haven't read since I was growing up. There is a queer touch of Tolstoi's creeds now and then. This copy was printed in '83, — how strange that I never knew anything of it!

Tonight I saw the dear little new moon through the elm boughs; and have read part of one of Hawthorne's American Journal volumes but didn't care for it as much as I used to. On the contrary, I found the "Rambles about Portsmouth" a mine of wealth. One description of the marketwomen coming down the river, — their quaintness and picturesqueness at once seem to be so great, and the mere hints of description so full of flavor, that it all gave me much keener pleasure than anything I found in the other much more famous book. This seems like high literary treason, but you wait and see. This was a volume of Hawthorne's younger journals, a conscious effort after material and some lovely enough notes of his walks and suggestions for sketches; but these last lack

[1] Whittier.

any reality or imagination, rootless little things that could never open seed in their turn, or make much of any soil they were put into, so "delicate" in their fancy as to be far-fetched and oddly feeble and sophomorish. You will find it hard to believe this without the pages before you as I have just had them. But oh! such material as I lit upon in the other book! one page flashes into my mind now as 'live as Kipling and as full of fresh air, and all the touches of brave fancy and quiet pathos. Let an old fellow like Brewster keep at it as he did, and he quietly brings you a ruby and a diamond, picked right up in a Portsmouth street. Such genuine books always live, they get filled so full of life : it 's neither Boswell nor Johnson who can take the credit, but the *Life* on the pages.

"Too useful to be lonely and too busy to be sad."

That is the most lovely thing that Miss Phelps ever said or wrote.

Thursday morning.

I shall have to write you the same sort of letter as Selborne's White wrote to the Hon. Daines Barrington, for there does n't seem to be anything to tell, except how things grow and what birds have come and how things

don't grow and what the birds do. There is
one adorable golden robin in one of the garden elms, who shouts " Pitty, pitty, *pitty!*"
all day long like a delighted child, — you will
be so pleased to make that cheerful bird's acquaintance when you come. (I don't feel very
certain about the time when I shall go to you.
It depends upon how much I can do today
and tomorrow, and it also depends upon how
things are here, and what news I get from
Judge Chamberlain, to whom I have been
writing about a desk at the Public Library.
But if I don't go Saturday, I certainly must
be no later than Monday, for I must get a
good deal done next week. I am trying to get
to a certain point in the story here, and then
be free to forget that part and to do the chapters about the cathedral, etc., while I am away.)
I can't say enough about the Ruskin biography. I can hardly wait to have you know
it, too. He is after our own heart in his affection for Dr. Johnson. Next week, if we have
some time for reading, do let us take some of
Mr. Arnold's papers that we have been putting
off, and some of the poems. It seems like cram-
ming, but I was so sorry I was not more familiar
with certain parts of his work when I saw him

before. But some things of his we know as
well as we know anything — thank goodness!

Yesterday I was busy both morning and
afternoon, and got on much better than the
day before, and I hope it will be the same today. I was reading "Two Years Before the
Mast" in the evening, with new admiration
for its gifts. It seems to me as much a classic
as anything we have to give, — it has excep-
tional charm in the way it is done, with perfectly genuine qualities. There is so little that
is usually thought interesting to tell, and yet
I could hardly skip a page.

What did you think of G. Sand's letter to
Madame d'Agoult, — that long letter at the
beginning of the book? I couldn't bear to
have you read it without standing by and seeing how you liked it. Nothing ever made me
feel that I really know Madame Sand as that
letter did.

Monday evening.

Such a heavenly day. I do wish that you
could have played out of doors in the sun as
I did. After dinner I stole away to my fence-
corner and spent a beautiful season of peace
and quietness. Jock followed me, but the dis-

tant sound of a gun scared him, and so he
crept close to my petticoats. I had my little
old "Milton's Shorter Poems" in my pocket
and read "Lycidas" with more delight than
ever before; and then I did nothing for awhile,
and finally took to aimless scribbling, and I
don't wonder that you so dearly like to do your
work out of doors. You never would believe
how beautiful the country looked; and yet
after a while I had a consciousness that something strange was going on, and looked up
to see a great white and grey trail of fog, like
a huge reptile all along the course of the river
past the town, and so I knew that there was
a noble sea-turn on its way inland, and scram-
bled to the top of the hill to find all the eastern country a great grey lake, Agamenticus,
hidden (for once, you will say), and in fact
the edge of the low cold cloud was uncomfort-
ably near, so Jock and I raced it home and
beat, for it was only a minute or two before
the village was all a mist.

Madame Blanc's picture came tonight, and
I forgot to tell you that a little note from her,
heralding it, came yesterday. She must have
given it to some friend to bring across. The
engraving is signed by Amaury Duval and is

very sweet to look at. When it was taken,
twenty years ago, she says it took the medal at
the Salon. I think it is a little large to bring
to you, but perhaps not.

Sunday evening.

I have got a little cold, so I stayed in most
willingly today, and have finished the Coleor-
ton letters. I long to have you begin them, or
to begin them over again with you. I suppose
that some or many of them must be printed else-
where, I am too ignorant to say; but Wordsworth's and Dorothy's letters are more delightful and wise and like their best selves than any
words of mine can say. Coleridge's, too, follow
his varying fortunes and ailments over hill and
dale. In Wordsworth's there is a delectable
account of his planning and overseeing a
"winter garden" for the Beaumonts, which I
hope we shall go to see, some day, and there
are particulars now and then about how the
evergreens grow, and he writes inscriptions for
it, and it is a great play! But Dorothy! how
charming she grows as one grows older and
learns to know her better. How much that we
call Wordsworth himself was Dorothy to begin
with. Wordsworth's letters so often make me

think of Mr. Arnold. He would love the book
— but I am in such a hurry to get you at it.

"Existence is the most frivolous thing in the
world if one does not conceive it as a great
and continual duty." I am so glad you told
me to read this, for I might never have gone
back to it of my own accord.

I have such a charming new book, the "Life
of William Barnes" the Dorset poet, by his
daughter. There is almost too much of his
own poetry sandwiched in, which delays the
run of the biography (to me) — not but what I
love some of the poems very much. He is like
the parish priest in the "Deserted Village," —
[with the wonder] "that one small head could
carry all he knew"! I think it would be a lovely
thing to make a paper for the "Atlantic" or
some of the magazines. If I had been to his
village, how I should love to do it, and there is
my priest of Morwenstow waiting yet! Perhaps
they will be nice things to do this winter?

(TO T. B. ALDRICH)

SOUTH BERWICK, MAINE.

You and I are such timid young authors
that I can now afford distinct reassurance,
and say with deep pleasure how much I like

your two new stories! You spoke slightingly
of " Shaw's Folly," but that was the folly of
T. B. It is done with such freedom of hand
and brightness of touch that I liked it most
uncommonly well, and the only shadow of dis-
satisfaction that a fond reader can find, is that
the writer did n't say what the cure might
have been for such a sad failure! I suppose
it is the old story, that we can't trust sentimentality to build houses, or rather to keep
them running on business principles. The distinction between sentiment and sentimentality
is a question of character, and is as deep as
one can go in life, and kindness must have a
sound tap-root. We are trying to speak of
model lodgings, rather than of literature that
depicted Mr. Shaw! We must go right to
A. F. to get straightened out! But I love the
way that you have written that story. *There's*
realism seen from the humorous point of view :
the trouble with most realism is that it is n't
seen from any point of view at all, and so its
shadows fall in every direction and it fails of
being art. "All of which is respectfully sub-
mitted," as they say in state papers.

The brilliant tale touches one's imagination
in the quickest way. I find that it keeps com-

ing to my mind as the " Two Boys in Black"
has kept coming these many long years. It
puzzles one as if it were one's own experience,
and that touch about the handkerchief on the
face, keeps insisting that the lady — what did
she do if she did n't die? But this is getting
to be a painful one-sided talk instead of a letter, and I must end it. I wonder if you are all
as happy as you were the other morning? I
feel as if I had looked in at the window and
seen you all by accident, and as if I must n't
even think about it myself! There is only one
word more: please keep on writing!

(TO MRS. FIELDS)

Saturday morning, 12 *October,* 1890.

I was busy writing most of the day yesterday, but went up the street for an hour to
the funeral of a little grand-child of one of
our neighbours. The mother had died of con-
sumption not long ago, and this delicate little
thing was brought to the old grandmother to
take care of. So it was a blessed flitting, and
a solemn little pageant of all the middle-aged
and elderly neighbours going to the funeral
and sitting in the room where the small coffin
was, and that old, wise, little dead face, which

made one feel one's self the ignorant child, and
that poor baby an ancient wise creature that
knew all that there was for a baby to know,
of this world and the next.

There is a quaint archaic touch in Louise
Guiney's poem to Izaak Walton, and I do so
like Craddock,[1] who takes time, and is lost to
sight, to memory dear, and writes a good big
Harper's story. So does Sister,[2] with one for
the "Atlantic" called Felicia; so does not
S. O. J., whose French ancestry comes to the
fore, and makes her nibble all round her
stories like a mouse. They used to be as long
as yardsticks, they are now as long as spools,
and they will soon be the size of old-fashioned
peppermints, and have neither beginning or
end, but shape and flavor may still be left
them, and a kind public may still accept when
there is nothing else. One began to write itself this morning called "The Failure of Mr.
David Berry"; I have written a quarter, and
it goes very well indeed, and seems to have its
cheerful points.

I read "Madame Bovary" all last evening,

[1] Charles Egbert Craddock is the *nom de plume* of Miss
Mary N. Murfree.
[2] Miss Murfree's sister.

though I only took it up for a few moments
and meant to do some writing afterward. It
is quite wonderful how great a book Flaubert
makes of it. People talk about dwelling upon
trivialities and commonplaces in life, but a master writer gives everything weight, and makes
you feel the distinction and importance of it,
and count it upon the right or the wrong side
of a life's account. That is one reason why
writing about simple country people takes my
time and thought. But I should make too long
a letter for this short morning. Flaubert, who
sees so far into the shadows of life, may
"dwell" and analyze and reflect as much as
he pleases with the trivial things of life; the
woes of Hamlet absorb our thoughts no more
than the silly wavering gait of this Madame
Bovary, who is uninteresting, ill-bred, and
without the attraction of rural surroundings.
But the very great pathos of the book to me,
is not the sin of her, but the thought, all the
time, if she *could* have had a little brightness
and prettiness of taste in the dull doctor, if
she could have taken what there was in that
dull little village! She is such a lesson to
dwellers in country towns, who drift out of relation to their surroundings, not only social,

but the very companionships of nature, unknown to them.

Was there ever anything so delicious as Carlyle's calling Margaret Fuller "that strange lilting, lean old maid!" I think "lilting" is too funny, and how many times do you suppose he "laffed" after he wrote her down? I never loved the Carlyles before as I do in this book. Don't you wonder at him more and more? Froude is always the lover of his heroes, but I can't help thinking he is only just to Carlyle. I wish we may have a chance to go to the Athenæum next month, and see some of the English reviews of the book. I want to read about it. The Carlyle makes other books seem trivial, as books, just now. That cross Scotchman seemed to carry an exact, inexorable yardstick, and to measure with it as if he were a commissioner from the Book of Judgment, though everybody else ran about with too short yardsticks and too long ones.

I think better of the Lord Houghton book, as I see it more, just as you did. What an exquisite letter that is of Tennyson's, when R. M. M. was cross at him, and what a *dear* kind old pat on the shoulder our reverend

Sydney Smith gave him, when R. M. M. thought he had been called names of the " cool of the evening," etc., etc. And I *do so* like Carlyle's first long letter, from Fryston to his wife.

Saturday afternoon, 17 *January*, 1891.

This is a short word for you to read on Monday morning, written at the close of a dark and stormy afternoon. I have been sitting in mother's room, reading your big Rumford book, which I somehow have taken into my head again. He was such a charioteer! What do you think that he did once but have every beggar in Munich arrested! and then sorted them out after careful examination, giving work to those who needed it, and helping all deserving, and dealing with the naughty ones. There was a huge work-house, for instance, where they were put at trades. You would be much pleased with the accounts, and some time we must talk about it. I have felt a little tired and clumsy-handed, and the Rumford book was just the thing. The count was really such an interesting man. Oh, if this young republic could have had his practical wisdom !

Wednesday night, *August* 12, 1891.

What sad news from Elmwood, dear! It
makes me so heavy-hearted to think of our
loss of such a dear friend, and of poor Mabel's
sorrow. What must not this lovely hot, bright
day have been to her! I don't know of any
one who could feel such sorrow more keenly.
I think and think of her, and so must you, I
am sure, and how we should talk about dear
Mr. Lowell if we were together. Here he is
only the "Lowell" of his books, to people,
and not a single one knows how dear and
charming he was, and how full of help to one's
thoughts and purposes in every-day life. I
wrote to Mabel most truly that I was as fond of
him, almost, as if I belonged to his household
and kindred. And I suppose that the last bit
of writing for print that he may have done
was that letter for me. I have been looking
over two or three of his letters or notes to me,
which I happen to have here, with such affection and pleasure. How you will like to look
over your great package! And how I treasure
that last time I saw him, and the fringe tree
in bloom, and Mabel gone to Petersham, and
he and I talking on and on, and I thinking he
was really going to be better, in spite of the

look about his face! I suppose you will go up
to the funeral; you must remember what people say, and every little thing that we should
care about together, to tell me. And yet I say
to myself, again and again, how glad I am that
the long illness is ended.

Saturday morning, SOUTH BERWICK.

And more sad news. Dear old Dr. Pea-
body gone, too! but let us be thankful that
he could enjoy life so long and so late.
Everybody remembers him here with such
love and gratitude, for the charming address
that he made two years ago. How many of
the little New England towns have such a
pleasant memory!

Don't you remember that somebody, while
we were away,—oh, it was Mr. Alden,—told
us how exquisite William Watson's "A Prince's
Quest" was? Last night, after I came from
my tea-party, I read most of it with great delight. I wish that we could read many of the
poems together, but I still cling to my first
love, the Dedication to James Bromley. This
is Saturday again, and I suppose you will have
your dozen of pleasant people come in. I love
the Saturday companies dearly.

(TO T. B. ALDRICH)

HOTEL BRUNSWICK, NEW YORK.

MY DEAR FRIEND, — I am writing this letter to thank you for your beautiful poem in memory of Mr. Lowell, — but how can I find words to say what I wish to say about it! To me it speaks of him as his own presence used to speak, and brings him back again as if he came back with the old life and the new life mingled, as indeed they are, and then I feel the loss afresh, and somehow wake from the reading of the poem to know how great and how lovely a poem it is, and to be prouder of you than ever, and of your always reverent and happy use of your beautiful gift. I wish that I could indeed tell you how much I thank you, and how straight this last poem has gone to A. F.'s heart and mine.

A. F. is reading " My Cousin the Colonel," and bursting into laughter now and then as one seldom hears her. I always say that she is a poor supporter of story-writers, but it is not true now that she can get hold of something of yours again.

We have had a delightful week, and it has been good for both of us. Day before yester-

day we had a great pleasure in Mr. Booth's
sending for us to come and have tea with him,
and then showing us all the Players' Club!
But every-day things have reminded me of
you and Lilian. We are to go home on Tuesday. Forgive this bad pen that writes so blun-
deringly what was in my heart to say, but I
cannot tell you with any pen how much I care
about " Elmwood."

(TO MR. GEORGE E. WOODBERRY)

SOUTH BERWICK, MAINE, 1 *November*, 1891.

MY DEAR MR. WOODBERRY, — I wish to
thank you most heartily for your essay upon
Mr. Lowell in the "Century." I do not know
when I have read anything with such delight
and admiration. I only wish that it had been
printed in spring instead of autumn, — but if
it comes too late for his own eyes to see, at
least the eyes of other Americans will read it
clearer now.

I hope that I shall see you some day. I
have always wished to thank you for the pleasure I have had in your use of your beautiful
gifts in poetry and prose, but this essay leaves
me more grateful than ever.

(TO MRS. T. B. ALDRICH)

SOUTH BERWICK, MAINE, *November.*

MY DEAR LILIAN, — When I went to Town
for Sunday, I thought that I surely should
find you in Mount Vernon Street, and I was
so much disappointed when I heard from A. F.
that you were still out of town, and especially that you are not quite well yet. I have
been expecting to go to Boston and to see
you there, so that I have never written you
a word! I was so grieved to hear of your illness, and I wish very much to see you. If I
possibly could have stayed I should have gone
to Ponkapog to spend an hour at least, — dear
Ponkapog! how I should like to have a drive
with you again!

I have been busy, as everybody is when she
first gets home after seven months and more
away, — answering foolish strangers' letters,
and so never having a minute in which to write to
wise friends, and trying to get a little writing
done, and trying to see all my neighbours, and to
remember which bureau drawer anything is in!
It was so sweet to get home again and into
the old places — I never shall forget the beauty
of that first evening on Charles Street as we

sat looking out over the river, and being so
glad to be off the steamer; and next day,
when I came here to the dear old house and
home, it all seemed to put its arms round me.
I am always looking forward to having you
and T. B. A. here. I wish it were not so late
in the autumn.

(TO MRS. FIELDS)

Saturday afternoon, 1892.

I long to have you get to the chapter
in Dr. James's book that I have been reading
to-day : " The Value of Saintliness." I "find"
it most particularly fine, and penetrating.
There is a good page or two about St. Teresa
in the *chapter before* which would do your
heart good to quote, — I mean now the first
paragraph as far as " It is a fine summing-
up."

The other day quite out of clear sky a man
came to Mary with a plan for a syndicate to
cut up and sell the river bank all in lots, —
and *oh* if Mrs. —— only does want to buy it,
or her friend, it will be so nice and make such
a difference to me. Sometimes I get such a
hunted feeling like the last wild thing that is
left in the fields.

In Gloucester.

When autumn winds are high.
They wake and trouble me
With thoughts of people lost
  A-coming on the coast;
And all the ships at sea

How dark, how dark and cold
And fearful in the waves
Are tired folk who lie not still
and quiet in their graves; —
  In moving waters deep
That will not let men sleep,
  as they may sleep on any hill;
May sleep ashore till time is old
And all the earth is frosty cold.
Under the flowers a thousand Springs
  They sleep and dream of many things.

God bless them all who die at sea! —
If they must sleep in restless waves
God make them dream they are ashore,
  With grass above their graves.

Sarah O. Jewett

CHAILLY, 9 *July*, 1892.

DEAREST ALICE, — Now they live in Barbizon, on the edge of the forest of Fontaine-
bleau, under the very eaves I ought to say,
and they are having a beautiful good time,
and in the day-time they play in the woods, and
after dinner they walk out on the great plain
and hear (and almost see!) the Angélus. I wish
I had time to write a long letter all about
Paris and Madame Blanc who brought us here.
I can tell you that I went up her stairs with
my heart much a-feared, — it is an awful ex-
periment to see so old a friend for the first
time, — but I found her even more dear and
kind and delightful than she has been in her
letters for those eight long years. There has
been no end to her friendliness, and what I have
liked very much, she has taken us to see some of
her friends, one ideal French lady, a comtesse
of the old school, in the Place Vendôme,
whose self and house together were like a
story-book. You would simply love the drives
here, but I dare say you know them much
better than I. Last night we strayed far out
on the great plain, and when we were coming

back I heard a man with his heavy scythe cutting the wheat, and it was so dark I could n't see him, and perfectly still, except the noise he made, — the sharp swish of the scythe and the soft fall of the grain; one could n't hear it so by day. When we hear the Angélus we can't help looking all about for two figures with bent heads. Millet's own house is close by ours. We have some rooms in a pretty old place, covered with vines ; you go out through a half court-yard and half farm-yard and open a big gate to the narrow paved street — and a nice piggy lives in a little stone mansion close by this gate. I feel very much at home, being in truth a country person, but nobody could help loving Barbizon.

> O little *pains !* Mes petits breads !
> I break with joy your crisp young heads !
> In you no dreadful soda lurks
> To stab me with a thousand dirks.
> Some baker immigrant should bring
> You to my New World suffering.

(TO MRS. WHITMAN)

22, Clarges Street, MAYFAIR, W.
LONDON, 20 *August*, 1892.

I believe that I wrote you last from Yorkshire, and there seems to be so much to tell

SARAH ORNE JEWETT
From a photograph taken by Frederick Hollyer in 1892

since, that my pen quite flies in the air, like a
horse that won't go. We had a lovely scurry
indeed, home from Ilkley by the way of " Lincoln, Peterborough, and Ely," not to speak
of Boston and Cambridge, where we gave ourselves just time enough to see Newnham, and
to have a walk and to go to the afternoon
service at King's College Chapel, and to stray
afterward in the dusk into Trinity Hall to see
the portraits, and then to our inn to sleep as
best we might, after a great day, and go on to
London in the morning. We spent eight solid
hours in the House of Commons, on Tuesday
night, to hear the great debate, and were flying about a good deal all that week, and at
the end we went up into Warwickshire to stay
with Mrs. Dugdale, a most charming visit in
a story-book country house, which we both enjoyed enormously ; and then by Oxford back
to London again, and this last week we have
been seeing much of the Arnolds, who have
come back to town, because ——'s father-in-
law, of the house of Kimberly, is in the new
government, and there was a revival of " society " for a brief space, by which we profited.
It is a very good time to take for being in
London, on the whole, but we have been spend-

ing nights and making days' journeys to the
neighborhood, and begin to feel that we are
not likely to see half enough of London itself.
But what can I tell you (with a common *Flying Scotchman* pen) of going to see my Lord
and Lady Tennyson, down among the Surrey
hills ! It meant a great deal more to me than
when I saw them before. I wish I could make
you know their wonderful faces. One goes
into their presence with the feeling of a former
age. I believe that I know exactly what I
should have felt a thousand years ago if I
were paying a friendly visit to my king ; but
it is the high court of poetry at Aldworth,
whatever one may say. My Lord Tennyson
was so funny and cross about newspapers and
reporters that I feel his shadow above me
even in this letter, innocent-hearted as I be.
He has suffered deep wrongs indeed ; perhaps
it is well that I can't write long enough to
tell you many delightful things that he said
and did (saying some of his poetry once or
twice in a wonderful way), except one which
belongs to you, — his complete delight in my
Japanese crystal, which he looked at over and
over, and wondered much about, and enjoyed,
and thought to find things in it. Was n't

that nice of you, S. W.? and you a-giving it
to me, and indeed so many people beside a
poet have liked me for it, and remember me
now as the person to whom it belonged. If I
could have given it to anybody in this world,
I could have given it to Tennyson then and
there; but No! and now I like it more because he liked it, a-shining in its silver leaves.

Yesterday we spent the day with Mrs. Humphry Ward, who has been ill for a while and
is just getting better. Somehow, she seemed
so much younger and more girlish than I expected, even with Ethel, her next sister, clear
and dear in my mind. Ethel was not there,
but Mrs. Huxley, and her father and his wife,
and Mr. Ward himself, for which I was very
glad. I long to have you know Mrs. Ward.
You would quite take her to your heart. She
is very clear and shining in her young mind,
brilliant and full of charm, and with a lovely
simplicity and sincerity of manner. I think of
her with warmest affection and a sacred expectation of what she is sure to do if she
keeps strong, and sorrow does not break her
eager young heart too soon. Her life burns
with a very fierce flame, and she has not in
the least done all that she can do, but just

now it seems to me that her vigor is a good deal spent. She has most lovely children. The young son was busy with a cricket-match, and we beheld a good part of it, and saw the charming old garden, and altogether it was a very pleasant day indeed, and held pleasure enough for two or three. Now that I have begun to tell things, I wish to write you a complete autobiography of two weeks, but all the other people and things must wait until I see you, except perhaps that I must tell you how wonderfully well Mary Beaumont looks and seems. This week we are going to Cobham, to stay a few days with dear Mrs. Arnold, who would touch you with her changed looks. She has grown so much older since that merry day when we went to the first feast at Old Place. She asks so affectionately for you, and is just as dear as ever. When you get this letter, I think we shall be staying up at Whitby, on our way to Edinburgh, seeing the Du Mauriers again, according to agreement, and other friends, and liking to go there because Mr. Lowell was always talking about it and was so fond of it. Then we go on to Edinburgh. See what a little place I have left to send A. F.'s love in, but here it goes. Good-bye, dear.

And then "Lady Rose's Daughter"! If you were here how much we should talk about it. *There* are splendid qualities of the highest sort. One says at certain moments with happy certainty that here is the one solitary master of fiction — I mean of *novel writing*. How is she going on at this great pace to the story's end? But one *cannot* let such a story flag and fail — there *must* be an end as good as this beginning.

(TO MRS. GEORGE D. HOWE)

AIX-LES-BAINS, Sunday.

DEAREST ALICE, — I have sent many thoughts flying your way, if I haven't sent any letters in all this time, but the baths are a great siege and seem to take all one's time and one's wits away together. (And I beginning this letter on a half-sheet unbeknownst, but going straight on, it being among friends.) We have hardly begun to take the countless drives and excursions about this lovely green country, and look upon the journey to the Grande Chartreuse as if it were beyond Moscow, somewhere on a *steppe!*

Did A. tell you what a perfectly beautiful time we had when we boldly ran away to

Chamouny?— or Chamounix?— whichever
way you spell it, because I always forget.
I never, never shall forget one bit of that
lovely day when we drove from Martigny
over the Tête Noire. A.'s dear birthday and
such weather, and such flowers (it is *sainfoin*,
that pink one that I asked you about), whole
fields of ladies' delights, and large double
buttercups, and harebells, and forget-me-nots,
and red things, and pink things, and yellow
things galore, and Solomon's seal, one sprig in
a ledge just to show that there was a piece of
everything, if you only stopped to look: blue
gentians withal, something like our fringed
gentians in October. . . . We went on up
and up that dear, high green valley, passing
cold little white-silky brooks; and every now
and then on the road we came to peasant
families with their flocks and herds chirping
and clanking, and all the children capering,
and the old grand-mother with her staff, going
up to the high châlets, to pasture for the
month of June. We had a lot of candy and
gave largess and left such a wake of smiles
behind us. I went shopping for it in Martigny at break of day. And the grass so
green and just in flower, and none of it cut,

and everybody so pleasant along that road,
and we being so pleasant and gay that we
kept getting out to have a little walk; the
air getting into our heads, and the great
peaks coming around other peaks' corners, to
look at us solemnly, and all the morning
clouds blowing away one by one, until the sky
was all clear blue, and when we got to
Chamounix, at night-fall, Mont Blanc was shining white, and the full moon right above it,
as if we had come to see at last where the
moon lived, and started from, to go up into
the sky. And next morning we had a long
walk, with the sky still clear, and we were all
alone in the biggest hotel and felt like prin-
cesses under the orders of a " retinue." There
were very few tourists to be seen, but all my
month in Interlaken (when I came before)
means less to me, I believe, than that day
going up from Martigny. And after all this
we came back as good as pie and went to
work at our baths again, and never minded
much about the hot weather or anything.
I somehow hate not to have you go to Egypt!
(You would tell about it so well and ascertain
the address of a pretty Rag Fair — all to my
own good and delight!) but *don't* go fum-

bling in dark pyramids or make up a little paper bundle of sand of the desert that was too interesting to throw away, and always has sifted out over everything! . . . I wish I had begun to tell you about Chambéry, of which we have had one glimpse; tomorrow we mean to go there again and to see Les Charmettes and the Grande Chartreuse. Goodbye, with dear love.

VENICE, Thursday morn, 1892.

DEAR NEIGHBOUR AND FRIEND! — I now say that we did go to Torcello, and it was so heavenly beautiful that I forbear to speak. Oh if you *only* had been along! Such sails, such towers, such islands; on the far edge of the sea such a blossoming bough of whitest elder against the blue sky! And we ourselves, going all the way with a sail, and I holding the stern-sheets. It was in stripes of red and orange, with blue corners to it, faded just right, and a kind little breeze served us even in the little canal that leads almost to the cathedral door. What can we say about it? there the stone shutters, the old lonesome, mysterious mosaics that stare in each other's solemn eyes through the shadows, the damp-

ness, the greenness, the birds that sing and
the droning bells. Well, when you wish to
give me a happy moment of the sweetest remembrance, just say Torcello, and back I
shall fly to it. There were haycocks on a bit
of green meadow, and there were children in
an old boat playing and calling and rustling
the bushes by the canal, and the old Cam-
panile looked as if it were made strong to
hold up the sky.

I had a good dear letter from home this
morning; new dog a treasure, but three of
the horses with coughs— Dick and Betty and
Susan! the distemper thought to be of no con-
sequence by John until Dick caught it!

(TO MRS. FIELDS)

HOME, SOUTH BERWICK, *October*, 1892.

How much we have felt in these last days
and how we can see his pathetic figure[1] and
his great dim eyes. I am so rich in the
thought of that visit, and I can truly say that
the one thing which made me feel most anxious to have you get to England this summer
was to make sure of your seeing him again,

[1] Tennyson.

and now you have seen him and I too, and it was a most lovely visit. The great dignity and separateness of his life comes clearer than ever to mind. He seemed like a king in captivity, one of the kings of old, of divine rights and sacred seclusions. None of the great gifts I have ever had out of loving and being with you seems to me so great as having seen Tennyson, and then I stop and think of Mr. Lowell and wonder if I ought to have been so sure, though that *was* a little different. But if somebody said come and see Shakespeare with me I could n't have felt any more or deeper than I did about Tennyson.

SOUTH BERWICK, *October* 29, 1892.

Town means that I should begin things over again, and here it is very idle, and most of the dear village neighbours have made their kind visits, and we can be alone in the long sunny afternoons. Yesterday, a dear little old woman, who rarely leaves her house, came in to see Mary and me. " I know *just* how you feel, dear," she said, " I have been through the same sorrow "; and I could see that it was present yet in her heart, and she almost ninety, and missing her mother still.

It was a most tender and touching little old face, — I wish you had been here to know the dignity and sweetness of her visit, dear quaint old lady, mindful of the proprieties, and one who had seen almost everybody go whom she had known in youth, or middle-age, even. I wish you knew some of the village people, — not the new ones, but those to whom in their early days Berwick was the round world itself.

(TO MR. DAVID DOUGLAS, EDINBURGH)

10*th November*, 1892, SOUTH BERWICK, MAINE.

MY DEAR MR. DOUGLAS, — I only wish I were near enough to make one of your household now and then. I console myself by thinking that we do not live either in a letterless world or one where the remembrance of the past pleasures of friendship need ever be anything but present joy. As I sat at your table it was something like being at home in the old days when I still had my dear father and mother with all their wit and wisdom and sweetness. Now my elder sister and I are often alone.

It is funny how everything here seems to concern itself with the World's Fair at Chicago! for one of our magazines — Scribner's — means to be first in the field with a Great Representative Number! and I am hurrying to finish a story for it — a May number, but the editors are already anxious about being behind hand.

Mrs. Fields has seen Dr. Holmes and found him pretty well, and full of delightful fun; bearing his years cheerfully, and drawing his old friends closer, as he lets the rest of the world slip away little by little. Whittier's and Tennyson's death touched him closely, and it happens that some other old friends of his went this autumn too. Mr. Curtis, and Mr. Samuel Longfellow, the brother, a biographer of the poet, and Dr. Parsons, an erratic man of real genius, the translator of Dante and a poet of no mean skill, who was one of Dr. Holmes's and Mr. Fields's friends — all this has been sad for the dear old doctor, but as I have said, he keeps very cheerful.

Dear Mr. and Mrs. Douglas! My best thanks for Dean Ramsay's and Felicia Skene's book and more for the thought.

Yours most affectionately.

(TO MRS. GEORGE D. HOWE)

SOUTH BERWICK, 12 *February*, 1893.

MY DEAR ALICE, — It seems a very long time since I wrote to you, but these have been the chief reasons : two bothering eyes that won't always go when I most wish them to, and the following achievements of my pen mentioned in order and by name !

"The Flight of Betsey Lane,"
" Between Mass and Vespers,"
" All My Sad Captains,"
" A Day in June,"
" A Second Spring,"
and " A Lonely Worker,"

besides two or three short little things to give away, of a dozen pages of writing each — all bran-fire new except the "Sad Captains," which I had written through before I went away, and have now done ever so much more work upon! Look at that for a combination of Idleness and a New England Conscience !

But if I have n't written, there have been few days when I have n't thought of you pretty often. I acknowledge to a pang of wistful homesickness when you first wrote from the Bristol, — you can't think how I love the thought of my weeks there in spite of illness and sorrow and everything. I wish I could go to the Pincio with you, and wait in the sunshine until twelve o'clock, to hear all the bells, — to see the great brimming fountains as I come away, — to be with you, to lose Beppi[1] behind the hedge and find him again, about twenty feet away, and to see the roofs of Rome! How one keeps and loves a morning like that last morning! . . . Do you bless yourself a-going into the Sacristy at St. Peter's, and ever think of me a-seeing the lovely Forlis. *That* was a great morning, and I was just trying to remember how that mosaic of lilies went together in the chapel pavement. Don't you know we thought that S. W. could do it in glass and you were going to sketch it out for her? I always wish that you had been with us that afternoon, when we went to St. Onofrio. It was the dearest, most revealing place to me. I suddenly understood, as I never had before, just why persons could make themselves quiet and solitary nests in such places, and never wish to go out into the busy world again. I love St. Onofrio better

[1] A little dog.

than any little church in Rome, and there's the
truth. I should have to look off and see hills
and mountains, whatever my meetin' privileges
might be! which comes of being brought up
a Maine borderer.

So you have been cold? It has been freezing here; the longest stretch of very cold
weather that I have known for years. I have
been here most of the time, but going to town
every two or three weeks, and last time I stayed
ten days, a great visit if you please. Everybody felt Mr. Brooks's death tremendously. I
have never seen anything like the effect upon
the city the day of the funeral — the hush, the
more than Sunday-like *stop;* the mighty
mourning crowd about the church, and in the
church a scene that thrills me now, as I think
of it. The light kept coming and going, — it
was a spring-like day, with a sky full of shining
white clouds, and on all the plain black hang-
ings S. W. had made them put great laurel
wreaths, with a magnificent one of red carna-
tions and green on the front of the pulpit,
that was like a victor's trophy. When the
coffin came up the aisle, carried shoulder high
by those tall young men, the row of grave
young faces, the white lilies and the purple

pall! — it was like some old Greek festival
and the Christian service joined together.
The great hymn as they went out again —
" For all thy saints who from their labours
rest "; the people beginning it as if with a
burst of triumph, and the voices stopping and
stopping, until hardly anybody was left to sing
at all, and all the people standing and crying
as if their hearts would break — you can't
imagine what it was ! But nothing has ever
been such an inspiration, — it has been like a
great sunset that suddenly turned itself into
dawn.

Yours most lovingly.

(TO MRS. WHITMAN)

SPRING HOUSE,
RICHFIELD SPRINGS, N. Y., 29 *August*, 1894.

I must write you out of loneliness and pretty
deep-down sadness tonight. I had a telegram
Monday morning that Celia Thaxter had died,
dear old Sandpiper, as was my foolish and
fond name, these many years. We were more
neighbours and compatriots than most people.
I knew the island, the Portsmouth side of her
life, better than did others, and those days we
spent together last month brought me to know

better than ever a truly generous and noble heart. When her old mother lay dying, she called her boys, and said, " Be good to sister, she has had a very hard time"; and it was all true. She was past it all when I was with her in July. Life had come to be quite heavenly to her and — oh, how often I think of Sir Thomas Browne, his way of saying, " And seeing that there is something of us that must still live on, let us join both lives together and live in one but for the other." I wonder if you know those islands? with their grey ledges and green bayberry and wild roses, the lighthouse that lights them and the main-land far enough away to be another country? I suppose you do. At any rate, her little book about them is another White's Selborne, and will live as long.

What a solitary place a great hotel can be ! I felt it (as I have n't before) yesterday, with the thought of Appledore in my heart. But there are sights of friends to say good-morning to, even if there are few to say good-night.

To tell the truth I have been a nice unfriendly kind of hermit these ten days, and have read the "Three Guardsmen" like an idle school-boy, and the petty routine of baths and things can take any amount of time, and I am by this time quite unexpectedly limber, a right hand for instance working well and proof now offered. But you know Charles Lamb said that his would go on awhile by itself, as chickens walk after their heads are off.

(TO MRS. FIELDS)

SPRING HOUSE, RICHFIELD SPRINGS, N. Y.

I wish so to see you tonight and long so for tomorrow and next day's letters to know about dear Sandpiper. It has been a very sad day to me as you will know. It seems as if I could hear her talking, and as if we lived those June days over again. Most of my friends have gone out of illness and long weeks of pain, but with her the door seems to have open and shut, and what is a very strange thing, I can see her face, — you know I never could call up faces easily, and never before, that I remember, have I been able to see how a person looked who has died, but again and again I seem to see her. That takes me a strange step out of myself. All this new idea of Tesla's : must it not, like everything else, have its spiritual side, and yet where imagination stops and consciousness of the unseen begins, who can settle that even to one's self?

(TO MRS. WHITMAN)

SOUTH BERWICK, MAINE, Tuesday.

DEAR FELLOW PILGRIM, — I now say that I never had such a beautiful time as on Tuesday of last week, when I came to luncheon at your House, and spoke of Mrs. Kemble, and of the day of the Shaw Memorial, and of other things with Mr. Henry Lee. One treasures the last of that delightful company and generation, as if they were the few last survivors of an earlier and most incomparable one. I look upon that generation as the one to which I really belong, — I who was brought up with grand-fathers and grand-uncles and aunts for my best playmates. They were not the wine that one can get at so much the dozen now! I write in great haste, but speaking from my heart and quite incompetent to use proper figures of speech in regard to this large and dear subject.

We must say things about the "Life of Jowett," — a very true and moving book. I somehow think of him and those like him as I remember an unforgettable phrase of T. Warton's, "The great fact of their love moved on with time."

SOUTH BERWICK, MAINE, Thursday morning.

DEAR FRIEND, — It is impossible to say how your letter has heartened me. I send you love and thanks, — it is one more unbreakable bond that holds fast between me and you. You bring something to the reading of a story that the story would go very lame without; but it is those unwritable things that the story holds in its heart, if it has any, that make the true soul of it, and these must be understood, and yet how many a story goes lame for lack of that understanding. In France there is such a code, such recognitions, such richness of allusions; but here we confuse our scaffoldings with our buildings, and — and *so!*

This I feel like talking all day about, if you were only here, — but I come down to my poor Martha : I thought that most of us had begun to grow in just such a way as she did, and so could read joyfully between the lines of her plain story, but I wonder if most people will not call her a dull story. That would be all my fault, and sets me the harder at work; the stone ought to be made a lovely statue. Nobody must say that Martha was dull, it is only I.

(TO MISS A. O. HUNTINGTON)

148 Charles Street, BOSTON, 15 *April*, 1895.

MY DEAR MISS HUNTINGTON, — I am very sorry that your first letter to me should have been lost or overlooked. I thank you for this second letter, which gives me much pleasure.

I am very glad that you like "Deephaven" and that your friend likes it too, and I send this little page which I have just copied for you to give to her, as you say that you should like to do. As for the characters, Miss Chauncey is the only one who was a real person, and I made the first visit to her one afternoon just as I have described. Very little of that chapter is imaginary (or of the chapter called "In Shadow"). I do not like the picture of her, because I remember her much more ghostly and not such a brisk and determined person as the artist drew. This Miss Chauncey looks much too aggressive, while the real one was most appealing and a little bewildered as you may imagine. However, I

like all the rest of the pictures so very much
that I ought not to find fault with Miss
Chauncey!

(TO MRS. WHITMAN)

Sunday, *September* 8, 1895,
THE ANCHORAGE, MARTINSVILLE, MAINE.

You would not think from this handsome
and large paper what a small plain bushy
corner of the world this letter comes from.
The golden-rod is all in bloom, and there is
a lighthouse (Monhegan) off the coast, and
the Anchorage is a nice story-and-half house
that stands in a green field that slopes down
to the sea. I sleep in a little back bedroom
whose window gives on a lane and a stone
wall and a potato field, where the figures of
J. F. Millet work all day against a very un-
French background of the pointed firs that
belong to Maine, like the grey ledges they
are rooted in. I don't think you would like it
very well unless you fell to painting and then
— Oh my! — I don't wish for you as I do in
most places — perhaps it is because the landscape is usually without figures — in spite of
the potato field. But oh! I have found such
a corner of this world, under a spruce tree,

where I sit for hours together, and neither
thought nor good books can keep me from
watching a little golden bee, that seems to
live quite alone, and to be laying up honey
against cold weather. He may have been idle
and now feels belated, and goes and comes
from his little hole in the ground close by
my knee, so that I can put my hand over his
front door and shut him out, — but I promise
you and him that I never will. He took me
for a boulder the first day we met; but after
he flew round and round he understood
things, and knows now that I come and go
as other boulders do, by glacial action, and
can do him no harm. A very handsome little
bee and often to be thought of by me, come
winter.

Did you read Bourget's address on his admission to the *Académie?* I have had it for
ever so long, waiting for the right day; there
was so much of the cramped newspaper type,
that wind, weather and the planets had to be
all right. It is wonderfully interesting, quite
a noble speech, I think, and quite his own
heart and hope talking out loud, as if there
were no people there. Thus he says once:
"Tant il est vrai que le principe de la création

intellectuelle comme de toutes les autres reside
dans le don magnanime et irraisonné de soi-
même, dans l'élan attendri vers les autres,
dans la chaleur de l'enthousiasme, et que le
génie de l'artiste est comme toutes les grandes
choses du monde : un acte de foi et d'amour."
Some day I wish we could talk about this address of Bourget's — there are things about it
which touch one's heart very much.

(TO MRS. FIELDS)

STONEHURST, INTERVALE, N. H.,
Tuesday night [1896].

Such a nice day — out all day up in the
Carter Notch direction, trout-fishing, with the
long drive there and the long drive home
again in time for supper. It was a lovely
brook and I caught seven good trout and one
small one — which eight trout - persons you
should have for your breakfast if only you
were near enough. It was not alone the fishing, but the delightful loneliness and being
out of doors. Once I was standing on a log
that had fallen across the stream, and I looked
round to see a solemn little squirrel who had
started to cross *his bridge!* and discovered me.

He looked as if he had never seen such a thing before, and he sat up and took a good look, that squirrel did, and then discreetly went back. You ought to have seen us looking at each other; *I* didn't know there was anybody round either!! I went off alone down the bed of the great brook, and was gone three hours, and the boys went off another way. It really did me good, and I got wet and tired hopping from stone to stone, and liked it all as much as ever.

(TO MISS ROSE LAMB)

Monday 11th, 1896, SOUTH BERWICK, MAINE.

MY DEAR ROSE, — I was in town again for a few days, last week; I mean week before last, and I thought of you and of Mrs. R——, but I was more taken up with affairs than usual so that I could not manage to get to see you. Now I am so busy with some writing here that I cannot say when I shall get to town again. But tell Mrs. R—— that the only way is to keep at work! If I were she I should read half a dozen really good and typical stories over and over! Maupassant's "Ficelle" for pathos and tragic directness, for

one, and some of Miss Thackeray's fairy stories, — "Cinderella," for instance, which I have
always admired very much, — old-fashioned
romance put into modern terms, and Miss
Wilkins's story about getting the squashes in
one frosty night, and the cats being lost! I
can't remember its name though the story
is so clear and exquisite to my mind, and
Daudet's "La Chèvre de M. Sequin" and
"La Mule du Pape." These are all typical
and well proportioned in themselves and well-
managed, and I speak of them because they
come readily to my mind, and give one clear
ideas of a beautiful way of doing things. One
must have one's own method : it is the personal contribution that makes true value in
any form of art or work of any sort.

I could write much about these things, but
I do not much believe that it is worth while
to say anything, but *keep at work!* If something comes into a writer's or a painter's
mind the only thing is to *try it*, to see what
one can do with it, and give it a chance to
show if it has real value. Story-writing is
always experimental, just as a water-color
sketch is, and that *something which does
itself* is the vitality of it. I think we must

know what good work is, before we can do
good work of our own, and so I say, study
work that the best judges have called good
and see *why* it is good ; whether it is, in that
particular story, the reticence or the bravery
of speech, the power of suggestion that is in
it, or the absolute clearness and finality of
revelation; whether it sets you thinking, or
whether it makes you see a landscape with a
live human figure living its life in the foreground.

Forgive this hasty note, which perhaps you
will read to Mrs. R——. I could not say
more just now if we were talking together.

Yours affectionately.

(TO MISS ELLEN CHASE)

9 *November*, 1896, SOUTH BERWICK, MAINE.

DEAR ELLEN CHASE, — How very good of
you to send me these nice photographs of
Whitby ! The face of the old woman is really
wonderful, with its eyes that have watched
the sea, — indeed every one is interesting. I
brought home a good many in 1892, and
wished for more, — but is it not delightful
that all these are new and different ? I am

very grateful to you, dear, for such kind thought. I knew Whitby first through Mr. Lowell, who used to talk much about his summers there : so that after he died, and I went there, the place was full of memories of him. Do you know (of course, you do) his letters about it in the Life that Mr. Norton edited ? I am sorry to say that Mrs. Fields overlooked one, in sending her letters to Mr. Norton, which is more beautiful than any : about grey St. Hilda's Abbey and the red roofs of the old town. And now as I look back I remember also how I went about the streets of Whitby with Mr. Du Maurier and his little dog, and one day I heard the songs in " Peter Ibbetson," with their right tunes sung by that charming voice that is silent now. So, with all this, you see that pictures of Whitby mean a great deal to me.

I am very glad to have the photograph of your own house. It looks as if it were old, and not new: it looks as if it were not without a past and dear associations, which is much to say of a new house. Some day — oh, yes indeed ! — I should like dearly to come and see it.

Yours very affectionately.

I wonder if you have not been reading "Sir George Tressady," — a really great and beautiful story as I think. I care very much for it.

(TO MRS. FIELDS)

Monday morning.

Yesterday I did n't go out, but finished the first volume of Edward Irving and then read Carlyle's truly wonderful paper about him, in which, by the way, he says that Mrs. Oliphant's account of Irving's last days is quite wonderful. He is really eloquent in writing about it, but finds the early part of the biography a little untrue to the character of Irving as he knew him, romantic and idealizing to some extent. You feel that what he says of their various interviews and associations is exactly as he knows it, and always most sympathetic and affecting, as you will remember; but to Mrs. Oliphant, Irving stands almost against the dark background of his fate. Irving seems less great than I expected, but very moving, a creature of brilliant natural gifts, especially of speech. He would have made a certain kind of great politician, perhaps after Gladstone's kind, but I understood part of the reason of his decline

when Carlyle says that he was not a reader.
Men of his impulsive nature ride off on strange
ideas when they fail in what Matthew Arnold
tried to teach in " Literature and Dogma."
After all, Irving failed through the mistakes
of ignorance, and a self - confidence which
always goes with that kind of ignorance.
How we shall talk about this most moving
book.

. Carlyle took no stock in Irving's wife, and
he is so solemn and regretful about the Gift of
Tongues and the squeals of a lady parishioner
one day when he was calling. The squint of
Irving's eye was a sign of something in his
brain.

(TO MISS SARA NORTON)

SOUTH BERWICK, MAINE, 23 *February.*

How delightful it was to see you! I cannot
help thinking that yesterday morning is a very
dear hour to put away and remember. I got
home at half-past three in the afternoon, to a
world of snow, which surprised me very much,
with the rain raining on it as hard as it can and
a general outlook toward a tremendous month
of March. Tomorrow we are looking for some

friends who mean to come down from town to look at the old house I have often told you about, and of which they had heard. I can't imagine a drearier moment, but there are the big elms high and dry, and some other attractions, and they must take their chances and make their choices. Berwick always seems a little sad, even to me ! in the wane of winter. The old houses look at each other as if they said, " Good heavens ! the things that we remember !" But after the leaves come out they look quite prepared for the best and quite touchingly cheerful.

August 5, 1897.

Just at this moment, instead of going on with my proper work of writing, I find that I wish to talk to you. This is partly because I dreamed about you and feel quite as if I had seen you in the night. I am at Mrs. Cabot's, — my old friend's, — and somehow it is a very dear week. She has been ill ever since I came on Saturday, but not so ill as to give her much pain or me any real anxiety. I sit in her room and talk and read and watch the sails go in and out of harbor, and she speaks wisely from her comfortable great bed while we have a

comfortable sense of pleasure in being together. I am very fond of this dear old friend,
and I always love to be with her. Besides, it
is a house unlike any other, with a sense of
space and time and *uninterruptedness*, which
as you know is n't so easy to find in this part
of the world. One hates to waste a moment in
trivial occupations — you might write an epic
poem at Mrs. Cabot's — that is, if you might
write it anywhere !

I think of the old house at home as I write
this so gayly, and to tell the truth, I wish that
you and I were there together. If we were
there we should see the pink hollyhocks in the
garden and read together a good deal. I wish
that my pretty dream were all true ! but one
finds true companionship in dreams — as I
knew last night.

Dear child, I shall be so glad to see you
again. I have missed you sadly this summer in spite of your letters, — in spite of time
and space counting for so little in friendship !

SOUTH BERWICK, 3 *September.*

It is so nice to direct your envelope to Ashfield, that I must speak of it to begin with !

Your last letter from London came yesterday and made me sorrier than ever, because I could not carry out my best of plans of going to town: I do so wish to see you! I wish that Berwick were on the way to Ashfield; but then one might as well wish for things that can come true.

This is my birthday and I am always nine years old — not like George Sand, who begins a letter — no, no! I mean Madame de Sévigné!! — "5 fevrier 16—; il y a aujourd' hui mille ans que je suis née!" If you were here I should just stop a long bit of copying and take a short bit of luncheon in a little plain basket, and you and I would go off at once up "the little river" to keep this birthday with suitable exercises. I have quite forsaken the tide river for its smaller sister this year, the banks are so green and all the trees lean over it heavy with leaves. You have come home at the end of the most beautiful summer that I have ever seen ; it is still like June here and impossible to believe that we are only two or three weeks from frost. I shall love to think of you in Ashfield.

And the partings, dear Sally ! oh, yes, I feel deep in my heart all that you say in your letter.

One feels how easy it is for friends to slip away out of this world and leave us lonely. And such good days as you have had are too good to be looked for often. There is something transfiguring in the best of friendship. One remembers the story of the transfiguration in the New Testament, and sees over and over in life what the great shining hours can do, and how one goes down from the mountain where they are, into the fret of everyday life again, but strong in remembrance. I once heard Mr. Brooks preach a great sermon about this: That nobody could stay on the mount, but every one knew it, and went his way with courage by reason of such moments. You cannot think what a sermon it was!

I have just been reading the life of the Master of Balliol, and finding great pleasure within. You knew, did n't you? how fond he and Mrs. Dugdale were of each other, and that he was the kindest of friends to her sons. There is little of this in the two big volumes, I suppose because she is not given to letter-writing, which the Master certainly was, — some of his letters belong almost to the level of our E. F. G., — or I must say *quite*, when

I remember some to Dean Stanley and to the Tennysons. But this is too long a letter for the busiest of hard-working mornings.

(TO MISS ELLEN CHASE)

SOUTH BERWICK, *September* 27, 1897.

DEAR ELLEN, — Thank you again, and then once more for my little lemon-tree, which is keeping me company again on the sunny window-seat here, close by my secretary where I write. It has had a happy summer in the shade of the lilacs (and yet not out of the sun all day), and at this moment it has not many leaves, but no end of little lemons !!! One of them is as large as the end of my thumb, — so we must not believe that so noble a lemon-tree condescends to the Berwick climate. It always gives me great pleasure, and I love to remember whence it came, with the delightful old associations that every lemon-tree must always have, and the pleasant new ones that you gave this special one.

(TO MRS. FIELDS)

SOUTH BERWICK, Wednesday afternoon.
[*After a visit at Mr. Whittier's house at Amesbury.*]

I longed to send you a note this morning,
but unluckily I did n't have any paper upstairs,
and had to leave soon after breakfast, or before half-past eight, so I did n't like to ask for
writing materials! I was so glad that I went.
"Thy dear friend" was so glad to see me, and
we sat right down and went at it, and with
pauses at tea-time, the conversation was kept
up until after ten. He was even more affectionate and dear than usual, and seemed uncommonly well, though he had had neuralgia
all day and made out to be a little drooping
with the assistance of the weather and coming
company. But oh, how rich we are with "thy
friend" for a friend! He looked really stout
for him, and his face was so full of youth
and pleasure and eagerness of interest, as we
talked, that it was good only to see him. The
LL. D. had evidently given pleasure, though
he was quite shy about it. He was full of
politics, but we also touched upon Wallace
and my old grand-uncle, whom he used to
know in Bradford, grand-father's brother; and

we talked about Burns and "thy friend's" "Aunt Jones," who believed in witches, and he told a string of his delicious old country stories, and we went over Julian Hawthorne and Lowell, and the President and Mrs. Cleveland, and I told him how Lowell's oration made me feel, and I don't know what, or who else, except you and your dearest one, for he talked about you both in a heavenly way — of your friendship and how much he owed to you.

(TO MRS. WHITMAN)

SOUTH BERWICK, MAINE,
Friday night.

DEAREST S. W., — I came home to a day or two of illness, the last fling of an officious hanging-on old cold, and here I am writing to you, a little more good-for-nothing than common, but mending, and with the tag end of Hope to hold on by. Even for me things go crosswise, which one cannot bear to say, and I won't say, after all, but send you love and beg to hold on fast to the only certainty in this world, which is the certainty of Love and Care. I can't help feeling that Mary Darmesteter speaks true, out of great pain and the deep places of life, when she ends that last book, " The true importance of life is not misery or despair, however crushing, but the one good moment which outweighs it all." I cannot say how often I have remembered this in the last month. The only thing that really helps any of us is love and doing things for love's sake. I wanted to send you some sprigs of box, but a flurry of snow fastened down its covering of boughs, — it's winter now, you know; but I 'll just tell you one thing, it's going to be spring and there 's not a great while to wait, either. Don't you forget it was I who told you this, and said good-night, as if we were together, with a kiss and a blessing.

Whenever you want the Darmesteter book, " Renan," send down to 148 for it. I meant to carry it to you. I am just reading Mrs. Oliphant's "Life of Edward Irving" with great delight. There is a wonderful piece of landscape in the beginning (like one of your own pictures), where the boy goes over the moors in the early morning to his Covenanting Church.

South Berwick, Maine,
Friday night, *late.*

My very dear Friend, — I have dared to look into the Tennyson Life, late as it is, and I believe that I have read the greater part of it, making believe that I was only cutting the leaves. "The longer I live," he says once, "the more I value kindness and simplicity among the sons and daughters of men."

I think the book makes him live again ; it was a wonderful face, and he was far and away the greatest man I have ever seen. There was a kindness and simplicity — oh, most beautiful! but a *separateness* as if he had come from another world.

But how the days fly by, as if one were riding the horse of Fate and could only look this way and that, as one rides and flies across the world. Oh, if we did not *look back* and try to change the lost days! if we can only keep our faces toward the light and remember that whatever happens or has happened, we must hold fast to *hope!* I never forget the great window. I long for you to feel a new strength and peace every day as you work at it, — a new love and longing. The light from heaven must already shine through it into your heart.

(TO MISS SARA NORTON)

SOUTH BERWICK, MAINE, 28 *October*, 1897.

All these days I have thought of you often.
It has been a hurried, unexpected sort of time
with me, and a general sense of nothing happening quite as it ought to happen, as if the
North Star had got just a little bit out of
its place toward the northwest. My eye just
caught sight of your little photograph of the
Levens Bridge, perched on some papers at
the back of my desk, and it gave a pleasing
reassurance of the stability of England, even
if the State of Maine has got joggled.

I have had to go to Exeter several times
lately, where I always find my childhood
going on as if I had never grown up at all,
with my grand - aunts and their old houses
and their elm-trees and their unbroken china
plates and big jars by the fireplaces. And I
go by the house where I went to school, aged
eight, in a summer that I spent with my
grand-mother, and feel as if I could go and
play in the sandy garden with little dry bits of
elm-twigs stuck in painstaking rows. There are
electric cars in Exeter now, but they can't
make the least difference to me!

In talking lately with S. W. E. (she has
great charm for me as I think you know) it
seemed while she was speaking that her love
for your mother had been growing all these
years instead of fading out as so many old
friendships do when one has gone away. As
I write this I remember a verse which always
touches me profoundly, —

> "Come mete me out my loneliness, O wind,
>   For I would know
>   How far the living who must stay behind
>   Are from the dead who go."

I am stepping upon very sacred ground when
I write about this, dear child, but it has quite
haunted me, that bit of talk with S. W. E.
She was thinking aloud, I believe, rather than
talking to me, and yet she told me a little
story about you in your childhood which
made me know you as I never have known
you before, in such a near sweet way. As I
grow older it has been one of the best things
in life to take up some of the old friendships
that my mother had to let fall, there is a
double sweetness in doing this, one feels so
much of the pleasure of those who seem to
see something of their lost companionship return.

Thursday night, 1897.

Today we went out to the desired Canterbury to the great Shaker convent, which I have long wished to visit: it is more like a monastery than Alfred, and in some ways more interesting. I found friends of our old acquaintances there and heard the Alfred news. This great group of old houses is on a high hill, quite Italian in its site, and the views of the great lower country and the mountains beyond are wonderful. The color was most splendid today, and the lights and shadows chasing each other from yellow maple to brown oak. It would be a perfect place to send children now and then, as we used to think at Alfred. I shall love to tell you about it. I was deeply touched at heart to find the old sisters knew my stories ever so long ago, and were getting up a little excitement about my being there. The girls and my cousins had a great day, but such days are almost too much pleasure for my heart to bear, — the pathos, the joy of those faces, the innocent gayety of their dull lives.

(TO MISS ROSE LAMB)

148 Charles Street, *February 5.*

MY DEAR ROSE, — How delightful above everything this last letter of yours is from Luxor! I am sure that the winter is doing you a great deal of good, but we miss you, and it makes me a little homesick when I catch a glimpse of your house with the blinds shut as I come and go along Charles Street. I love to think that you are away, and especially that you are going to be in Athens by and by. Do not forget to look at my dear lady in the most beautiful of all the "grave reliefs" — no. 832: she is really the most beautiful thing in the world, and always a real person to me, so that the thought of her almost gives my heart a little thrill — 832 — *don't* forget her! This last fortnight Mary and I have both been here, and we have been going out so much that yesterday I protested against behaving like a *bud* any longer and told my sister that she must go home and let us settle down! I have really enjoyed going about and seeing people so much, — it is the first year in ever and ever so many that I have not had a heavy piece of work on hand, and I begin to see how often I have "gone out" feeling quite light-headed and absent-minded, after a day's writing; a very poor sort of guest, one must confess.

The photograph[1] is a delight — so great a type! I look and look at him. What distinction there is when you see that straight-lined figure among other photographs. I happened to put it with some modern things, and felt as if I must take it right away. Thank you so much, dear.

(TO MISS SARA NORTON)

BUCKLANDS HOTEL, Brook Street,
Grosvenor Square, W. 19 *April*, 1898.

I have seen all your primroses today and thought of you, too! Devonshire and Somerset were all a-bloom, and the brooks were fresh, and I heard a black-bird as the train went by, and I saw by this morning's Plymouth paper that the cuckoo had come and been heard in Brixham; which sounded homelike, because Brixham is a parish of the town of York next Berwick. And the fields were green and the trees showed all their lovely outlines under a mist of brown buds and small green leaves.

[1] Of the Charioteer at Delphi.

They never will be so lovely again all summer. Oh, yes, I thought of you, dear! and it really seemed at one moment as if you were looking out of the car window with me.

It was a dull voyage and I rejoiced when it was ended, though I never had so much fresh air as on this new big steamship which brought us over. That is saying much, but going to sea is going to sea in spite of everything. This time I read almost constantly, which one cannot always do at sea, and I liked very much coming into Plymouth, and spending the night there, and walking on the Hoe this morning, with thoughts of Sir Francis Drake and other great persons; but most of all of my poor great-grand-father, who was so unlucky as to be taken by privateers and shut into the wretched prison at Dartmoor, to know all the horrors of those dark days. You will know how eager we were to get news from home, and how disappointing it was to find that nothing was yet settled and that war still seemed near.

ST. RÉMY EN PROVENCE, 16 *May*, 1898.

I send you a leaf that you will know from this most lovely place, and whereas I last

spoke of primroses (I am sorry to think how
long ago!), I can now speak of the golden
lilies of France, which grow wild along these
roadsides, and scarlet poppies and young vine
leaves and old mulberry-trees, that look rue-
ful as if they thought it very hard to put
out nice leaves every year with the other
trees, only to have them picked for silk-
worms. Provence is in full flower and leaf
otherwise. We have seen a good bit of it,
with several days at Avignon, and some good
drives across country. I wish that I could
have had you with me one long day, when
Miss Travers and I went on pilgrimage to
Grignan, where Madame de Sévigné spent
her last days with her daughter, and died at
last, and was buried. It took us eleven hours
to make the not very long journey from
Avignon and back again (a rainy morning
forcing us to give up a drive and wait for a
branch train instead), and we had only half
an hour to see the ruined château and exquisite old French gardens; but it was one
of the most delightful things I had ever done.
The château rises high out of a lovely green
plain like a very small Orvieto, and a solemn
little old tiled village clusters under it, with a

tiny market-place where Madame de Sévigné
sits in her best clothes and her best manner,
so gay, so Parisian, so French, so enchanting
and so perfectly incongruous! You feel as if
it had not been kind to make her permanent
in bronze, — that some of the crumbly lime-
stone of the village would have been a kinder
material by far, except that it is, after all,
the crumbling old village that must some day
go, and she forever stay. Her little garden,
under a bit of high wall, with the fig-tree she
writes about, are still there as if she had
left them yesterday. The pastures were all
covered with thyme, in bloom just now, and
the air was blowing down from the snow
mountains which shut the valley in; and after
the wind and rain of the morning, the sun
had come out and cleared a blue sky like Italy.
One thinks of Italy always here. I have left
myself no time or room on this crumply sheet
of paper to tell you of a most enchanting *farandole* which we saw yesterday, in a village near
by, where all the dancers of different parishes
had come together. There was never anything
more exquisite than the whole thing, — the
open arena with the afternoon light through
the trees and all the country people so gay, so

delighted. The costumes and the *grace* of the whole thing; the Provençal dance-tune would have delighted you.

(TO MRS. WHITMAN)

Nîmes, 20 *May* [1898].

DEAREST S. W., — I have been thinking letters to you and not writing them, — you will have to take my word for it, there being no other sign. We have been loitering through this lovely country of Provence, with its young vines and its old olive trees, and we have lived in Avignon and at St. Rémy and spent an afternoon with M. Mistral, who lives in a great house behind fields of grain and grass and poppies and rows of mulberry-trees and grey olives like his own Mireio. And as you drive along the road to go and see him, golden lilies of France grow in the brooks, and beyond the hedgerows there are acres of big white poppies, — a crop of white nuns, one might say they looked like, all standing in pious rows in the sun. But of all the things I have seen, I wished for you the most to see those of yesterday. I was walking along a shady road by the riverside, above the Pont du Gard (that masterful old Roman ruin, which you must know better

than I did before I came). It was a very shady
road, and the only travellers besides A. F. and
me were nightingales, singing most cheerful
and rustling in the branches overhead. And
now just let me tell you something : the underbrush was *box*, growing in great bushes,
and the air was about as sweet as it could be
with that dry, strange, sweet, old scent that
tries to make you remember things long before
you were born. And we went walking on, and
presently we came to great gates, and still
walked on with innocent hearts and a love of
pleasure, and we crossed a moat full of flowers
and green bushes, and the other side of the
old bridge, beyond two slender marble columns with exquisite capitals, was another
gateway and a courtyard and an old château
asleep in the sun. All the great windows and
the hall door at the top of the steps were
open, and round the three sides and up to the
top of the tower green vines had grown, with
room enough to keep themselves separate, and
one of them near by was full of bees, and you
could hear no other sound. It was La Belle
au Bois dormante. You just kept as still as you
could and looked a little while, and came away
again. And the stone of the château was red-

dish, and the green was green, and the sunshine was of that afternoon softness that made
the whole sight of the old house flicker and
smile back at you as if you were trying hard
to look at something in a dream. It was in a
lovely corner of the world, far out from any
town. As we drove back to the — *world,*
we came over high pasture lands, where wild
thyme was growing (own cousin to the box
in the woods), and we could look off at little
high brown cities on the hills with one cam-
panile, as if they had been cities in Italy. And
one day, from Avignon, I went to the old
Château de Grignan, where Madame de Sévigné
used to come to stay with her daughter, and
where she died at last and was buried. The
château was ruined in the Revolution, but
there is the dear lady's little garden, as if she
had gone to heaven and left it only last year.
Her fig-tree, that she writes about sometimes,
looks very flourishing, and all her wallflowers
are tumbling over the battlements like a brook.
I shall have a great deal to tell you some day
about Château de Grignan. Wild thyme grows
in that country too. It is a very, very out-of-
the-way corner of the world, and we were all
day getting there and getting home again to

Avignon. And, besides all this, we have seen
Arles and seen Tarascon and other towns of
Provence, and we saw a *farandole* a-dancing
on a happy Sunday afternoon.

I am beginning to feel better than when I
came away, and things are getting on well,
and so far, for a rainy month of May indeed,
we had considerable pleasant weather. And
all this French sight-seeing is full of delight,
as you know, and I cannot forget.

Good-bye, darling! I think of you pretty
often, and I was as glad to get your letter in
Avignon (*most* as glad) as if you had come
walking in yourself. Tell me about the great
window, for indeed I try very hard to see it
as it goes up into place.

LA FERTÉ SOUS JOUARRE, SEINE ET MARNE,
6 *June*, 1898.

DEAREST S. W., — It is almost like getting
home, to find myself here with Madame Blanc
at last; and this day is A. F.'s birthday, and
the big fountain is making all the noise there
is, and all the birds are singing in the big-
walled garden, and beyond that, from my window in a little room out of my bedroom, where
I can write you a letter, one can look off over

the most lovely piece of French country: a long slope of a hill going up to the sky, muffled in green trees, with here and there a line of grey wall, or the sharp gable of an old farmhouse. And an interruption to the green with a piece of old weather-beaten red tiling of a roof. Which is to say that this is a quiet corner of old France, and the oldest bells in the world ring now and then very sweet and far off. Thérèse says that they sound as they do because they are the other side of the Marne, and " have to come through the water"! At any rate they are like a dream of bells, and I heard them first early on Sunday morning, yesterday, when I waked up.

The old town of Jouarre is on another hill, a mile or two farther down the river, and there is a square tower of the convent as old as the time of Charlemagne. Meaux is between us and Paris, with the grave of Bossuet in the cathedral, and beyond us is Rheims. As for Aix, it was as amusing and oddly English as ever, and I found my old friends all alive, — the funny old peasant women at the baths and in the market, with their brown smiling faces and white caps. I went to the Grande Chartreuse again, that lonely place in the

mountains, and slept in a cold convent cell,
and thought that the cliffs overhead might
tumble down in the night. It is a wonderful
piece of France, and when one thinks of disappointed lovers and courtiers going there to
end their days, and to keep silence and wear
the white Cistercian habit, of their leaving the
Paris of that day for the Grande Chartreuse,
it seems something amazing — human enough,
one may say, but first a refuge and place of
comfort, and then a prison and place of long
despair. I wish that you could see it as one
comes to it up the long, deep, forested valley,
with its gay light tourelles and peaked roofs,
as unexpected against the solemn mountain-
side as the statue of Mme. de Sévigné that
I told you about in the grim little place at
Grignan; but when you get nearer there are
terrible walls, and you feel that many a heart
has broken behind them, in winter weather
and loneliness.

(TO MISS SARA NORTON)

LA FERTÉ SOUS JOUARRE,
SEINE ET MARNE, FRANCE, *June* 6 [1898].

I am writing all my address at the beginning, because I am to be here for five or six

weeks (I hope!) with occasional flights to Paris
and to Rheims and so on,—and I think in
that time you will be finding time to write
to me how it looks in Ashfield. I was very
glad to get your letter, but it made me wish
that you were here, too. I felt sure as I read
that you were tired with that early summer-
tiredness, that belongs to New Englanders of
the old stock. I think there are moments
when one is sure that we have not had time
even yet to get acclimated, and the spring
weather in Old England has a kind of heredi-
tary ease for us, and superiority. I am a
grand-child of Mary Chilton, who came to
Plymouth (like half the old-fashioned persons
of Massachusetts and Maine!), but I can wilt
in a May sun as if I had just landed.

When I read your letter again, just now,
there was not a word in it that told me how
you felt, but I have long believed that one
folds up a bit of what we are pleased to call
personal atmosphere into one's note-paper and
that it always gets safe to the journey's end.
It is a fresh cool day here, with a lovely
French sky and bright sun, and this is such
a lovely place! I am delighted to be with
Madame Blanc, and it is almost like coming

home. You would like the old walled-garden,
with its "pleachèd walks" and great fountain,
and prim box - borders, and the dwarf fruit
trees with young fruit, and the bird's nest
where the bird is "anxious when you look at
her, but *not* frightened enough to fly away,"
as Madame Blanc said yesterday. The nightingales twitter and talk a good deal by day,
and at the foot of their garden you can un-
lock a door and find yourself in a country
lane that leads up the long slope of a great
green hill. There are two dear little brown
hunting-dogs — bassets — who live like lords
in a neat yard at the garden foot, by this
same door, and you can take them with you if
you watch them well, and remind them not to
kill marketable chickens at the first farm-house.
This is a country of wide views; you see three
or four brown villages at a glance; two of them
have only a couple of fields to separate them,
but I suppose when a person marries and
goes to the other village it is like going among
strangers altogether, just as they say good-bye,
almost forever, when they marry in another
island in Venice. You see that I have great
pleasure in being here. One loves a bit of real
country, or else one is indifferent, — it is much

more exciting to know a new piece of country than to go to a new large town.

10th of June. I am afraid that this long and dull beginning of a letter had better be torn in two, but I have only time to write half a letter, and not a whole one, before the post goes out. I wish that I could take you to see the brown old town of Jouarre, on a hill near here, with one of its convent towers as old as Charlemagne's time, and a curious old crypt, covered in the days of the Revolution and forgotten, and then rediscovered some years ago. There are some wonderful old tombs of the lady abbesses, and one of them was a young Scottish Princess who looks as if she had just climbed to the top of her high tomb and fallen asleep there, — a most dear and touching shape, — so young that time itself has looked on all these years and never laid a finger on her, or a troubling thought of age. Then, in a very old little church close by, is some old glass. One bit of a window is King David playing on a harp, and I am sure that you would say that it is exquisite as it can be in colour and feeling, and the sense it gives of great rapture, as with music. I long for some kind of copy of it to

take away; if ever you can find an afternoon
to spare in Paris, you must come to see so
beautiful a thing. I cannot forget it; but
all this beauty is in a corner of an old grey
village church, where the windows have been
mended with glass of another sort, and hardly
anybody comes from the outside world. Madame Blanc had long ago discovered this
wonderful old window with the King David,
and was so glad when we found it, too, and
cared about it as she did. I wish that Mr. Ruskin could have seen it and written about it.

I have not left myself half room to tell you
of some old French ladies, who interest me
very much. There is one — Madame de Beaulaincourt — who is the subject of much affectionate delight! She is the daughter of the
Maréchal de Castellaine, who was a famous
soldier in his day, and this dear person is a
great soldier, too, by nature; with a wonderful
distinction and dignity as she sits in her house
with all her old portraits, and (I am sure) some
friendly ghosts who come and go and remind
her of great French histories of courts and
camps. She was the friend of Madame Blanc's
mother, and is very fond of my friend. One
so easily can see *today* in a strange country,

but *yesterday* is much harder to come at, — so that I delight in going to some very old houses in Paris, and especially to Madame de Beaulaincourt. But La Ferté and the garden, and the old church bells, and the towers of Jouarre, are very hard to leave.

I hope now, more than ever, for some better news of the war. I feel quite as you do, but I think I can see better and better every day that it was a war which could not be hindered, after all. Spain has shown herself perfectly incompetent to maintain any sort of civilization in Cuba, and things are like some sultry summer days, when there is nothing for it but to let a thunder-shower do its best and worst, and drown the new hay, and put everything out of gear while it lasts. The condition is larger than petty politics or mercenary hopes, or naval desires for promotion, or any of those things to which at one time or another I have indignantly "laid it." I feel more than ever that such a war is to be laid at the door of progress, and not at any backward steps toward what we had begun to feel was out of date, the liking for a fight. I think that it is all nonsense to talk about bad feeling here in France, as it is certainly in England; for however people deplore the war in general and pity Spain, they generally end by saying that it was the only way out — that we *had* to make war, and then we all say that it *must* be short! If we could drown a few newspapers from time to time, it would keep up our drooping hearts and make us willing to bear the hearing of foolish details, and even painful details. It seems like a question of surgery, this cure of Cuba — we must not mind the things that disgust and frighten us, if only the surgery is in good hands. You know how much I saw of those islands two years ago? I cannot feel that the natural conditions of life are hard in the way they can be hard to poor Russians, for instance : a West Indian cannot freeze — he is impatient of clothes — he can pick a good dinner at almost any time of year off the next bush. But he can suffer in other ways, and Spain has made Cuba suffer in those ways far too long.

But how long I am writing these small thoughts about great things! You will say as the Queen did once in old times about Gladstone, — "He speaks to me as if I were a public meeting." Forgive me, dear Sally, and remember that I shall not be writing about the war again!

(TO MISS LOUISA DRESEL)

14 *June*, AIX-LES-BAINS.

MY DEAR LOULIE, — I wonder if Pyrmont
was anything at all like this! I remember it well
enough in your letters to feel that there were
more differences than likenesses; but a foreign
bath-town is a foreign bath-town! and this
amuses me a good deal. The rich and illustri-
ous English have their season just now and
are very interesting, for the most part, to me;
the dignified elderly men and the fine women
and charming tall girls, all have a refinement
and kind of perfection of development and
reasonableness, a repose and decision that I
like to watch very much. They are so unconscious and nice when they start off for a walk,
and wear such an air of satisfaction and triumph as they return. Later the French and
Spanish bathers come, — they are already beginning to appear, and are *très gais* as you
may suppose.

We know very few people here. Our dear
friends, the Edmundses, are most companion-
able, and Mrs. Parkman Blake is a near neighbour, and most kind and simple and friendly
always. We have had some little drives and

long ones together. She is going away soon
I am sorry to say.

I liked your letter from the country. I
always find Pepperell very interesting when
you go there. I keep stopping in my letter,
because a funny little Polish dame is playing
Rubinstein downstairs. She plays pretty finely,
too, though not so well as she must have
played before her fingers got quite so old, and
she is n't very clear about what she means,
or rather what Rubinstein meant, when she
comes to some places in the music. Still, a
great deal of feeling comes up the crooked
stairs in the notes. She is a cross-looking person in a funny blonde wig, and has very bad
manners at table, and has a funny way of
holding her head over her plate like a hungry
kitten, until you expect to hear a handsome
pin that she wears clink against the plate,
like the aforesaid kitten's padlock! This is
very wicked of me, but we are pretty friendly
nevertheless, and I write in a grateful spirit
for her good music. I wish you could see
her, Loulie! She looks as if she were born in
the far edge of Poland, or wherever it was
she came from, but had dwelt much in Paris
and always by herself, with not even a fel-

low kitten for company. It is a great temptation to write in this spirit about people you
don't know, just as I always laugh at everybody I choose at a circus — you don't feel exactly as if they had personality when you don't
know them, and feel as if they were figures
merely. "They ain't *folks*, they 're nothin' but
a parcel of images," an old friend of mine used
to say, with some truth, — but the minute you
get beyond a certain point of interest and
acquaintance, how this all changes ! — I find
myself beginning to think of new story-people
in these days, partly because having had two
or three of my sketches printed has made
me remember that part of me with surprising
vividness. I wonder if you won't look up the
June — no *May* — "Ladies' Home Journal,"
and read " An Every-day Girl " ? I think there
are good things in it, and I hope it will make
two or three things a little plainer to some
girls who will read it. Good-night, little Loulie. I must put down my pen now, but I have
enjoyed this bit of gossip. Love to your
mother.

(TO MRS. WHITMAN)

ST. MALO, 3d *July.*

I have been wishing to write to you ever
since the day I went to Rheims from La Ferté,
because I feel a little as if I had almost seen
you there. Whether a little wind that blew
against you when you were there, is still flickering among the pillars of the cathedral or
not, who can say ! but I think we went in together and I found something of you at every
turn. It was a surprise of companionship, with
all that surprise of beauty and strange solem-
nity which made me feel as if I had never
seen a cathedral — even a French cathedral
— before. Dear friend, I went at one step
much nearer to you than ever before, and
who shall say why ? It will be all the same
and hardly the less dear, even if you say that
Rheims was the one great cathedral that you
missed.

Since then we have spent the last days of
our visit at La Ferté, and one night in Paris,
and then started westward to spend a fortnight or so in Brittany before Mary and Theodore come to Paris. First we continued the
Madame de Sévigné pilgrimage by going to

Vitré to see Les Rochers, where she lived so much and wrote so many of her letters. I feel now as if I knew her very well, that dear lady, and as if her old orange trees were mine and the pretty echo in the garden. " She is always new like the spring," as Edward Fitzgerald wrote once. Vitré itself is an enchanting old town, and the green country most beautiful about it, — it was a day of great white clouds, like one day when you saw the Hamilton house!

We went to Mont St. - Michel from Vitré, and found it a most perfectly satisfying place ; even after all we had read and heard of it, we could not believe our own eyes when they saw such beauty — not only the mount itself, but the wide grey sands with their ribbon of sea-water and the rushing tides.

ILKLEY, YORKSHIRE, 30 *July*, 1898.

I long to tell you how much I love this Yorkshire country, the Bolton Abbey of Wordsworth's " White Doe of Rylstone," and Wharfedale, with its green fields that touch the sky, and its great brown moors, full of brooks and springs and peat-bogs and grown thick with budding heather, like fur on their long backs. We have climbed them as far as we could and driven over them, footing it bravely when the carriage could hardly be pulled with us in it. On the top the air is the sweetest and coolest air in the world. You follow the old road through the heather and fern and see the whole sky for once, and the moor, and nothing else.

Today we went to Haworth and found it most appealing. People had said that the Brontë church was pulled down and the rectory all changed, and that a railroad went to the town, which had set up manufactures and grown to 6000 inhabitants; but we sagely remembered such advices about other places. There were those who told us that there was nothing to be seen at " Les Charmettes." So we went to Haworth, and it is true that the church is a good deal bedizened, that the rectory is a little modernized, most of all that the present vicar resents pilgrims to the shrine of the Brontë family, but he did n't bite us. It is a dreadfully sad old village. The moors are n't so kind and sheltering as at Ilkley, here, but farther back from poor Haworth, and the plaintive sound of the old chimes will haunt my ears for many a day. You go up a long steep narrow street to the top of a hill. It all

looks pretty much as it did when that household, known of the world now, burned their
lights of genius like candles flaring in a cave,
like will o' the wisps of their upland country,
shut up, captives and prisoners, in that gloomy
old stone house. Nothing you ever read about
them can make you know them until you go
there. I can see the little pale faces of those
sisters at the vicarage windows ; and the Black
Bull Inn, where the strange young brother
used to comfort himself with light and laughter and country revelry, and break their hearts
at the same time, is a little way down the
hill. Never mind people who tell you there is
nothing to see in the place where people lived
who interest you. You always find something
of what made them the souls they were, and
at any rate you see their sky and their earth.

EDINBURGH, 11 *Sept.*

I wish I could possibly tell you anything
of the charm of Whitby. No wonder dear Mr.
Lowell grew so fond of it, and of the people
who spend their autumns there. We saw a
good deal of the Smalleys and Du Mauriers,
until we felt like oldest friends. You may expect me to be always telling you how delight-

ful Mr. Du Maurier is. You can't think of him at all until you see him and hear him sing his old French songs, and have him show you his drawings with all the simplicity of a boy with a slate, and all the feeling of a great artist. He is sadly troubled with his poor failing eyes now, but there is always a lovely sunshine in his face, and you meet him out walking with a timid little fluffy terrier that gets frightened and stops all of a tremble, and has to be hunted up just when his master is talking most eagerly, and turned back for, — such a beloved and troublesome little dog.

Whitby is full of pictures. There were places that made me think of your Gloucester picture, only a greyer sea and bright red-tiled roofs, climbing the steep hill, and a grey old abbey at the top of the hill, holding up its broken towers and traceries against the clouds. It is a noble seacoast and a most quaint fishing-town, quite unchanged and unspoiled. I shall be telling a great deal about the charms of Whitby.

I forgot whether I wrote you just before, or just after, our visit to Cobham. No, I am sure I have not told you about Mr. Arnold's favorite walks and his most interesting study, or

how delighted I was to find your own rhodo-
dendrons hanging on the wall.

(TO MISS SARA NORTON)

SOUTH BERWICK, MAINE.

MY DEAR SALLY, — It was too bad about
your missing Lady Macbeth. I wished much
for you, and indeed Madame Modjeska was
unexpectedly fine, — quite nobly beautiful.
She did two or three things which I must put
among the very best I have ever seen on the
stage. One felt true greatness in her playing.
I used to think of her as quite charming and
most intelligent and often vigorous, but she
went far beyond all these that night. You
would have cared very much for her, — but
alas, one must miss such pleasures. I don't like
to think of your losing a day now and then,
dear, except that there must come a " break "
and a Sunday, somehow ! I don't know what
we should do if we were not stopped by force
now and then, — the scheme of our life is
built on unending activity, or else an active New
England conscience falls to upbraiding us.

I have been busy enough since I came home,
chiefly here at the old desk. There are a great

many birds already, robins and song-sparrows
have all come, but there are some old snow-
drifts sitting round on the hills to keep watch.

(TO MRS. WHITMAN)

S. Y. Hermione,
NASSAU, Wednesday, 16 <i>January</i>, 1899.</div>

And I a-writing to a friend on a pleasant
summer morning and wishing that we could
have a word together. Two days ago I was
ready to change places with the coldest old
hurdy-gurdy woman that ever sat at the State
House corner, and nobody cared whether the
Gulf Stream was blue or whether it was pink;
but yesterday I waked up in Nassau harbour
and all was well, and we went ashore to
luncheon, and life seemed to begin with flying colors. It is a charming little town along
the waterside, with its little square houses
with four-sided thatched roofs; and down the
side lanes come women carrying things on
their heads, firewood and large baskets of
grapes, and an idle man-person on a small
donkey, and little black darkeys, oh, very black,
with outgrown white garments. I think it is
a little like Italy, but I suppose it is really
more like Spain. And I who write you have

seen cocoanuts a-growing, and as we drove along the bushy roads, A. F. did so squeak aloud for joy at every new bush and tree and tame flower a-growing wild. And when I found how easy it is to get here all the way by rail to Florida, and across from Palm Beach (Jupiter Inlet) in a day, I wonder that more people don't come to this charming Victoria Hotel among its great silk-cotton trees, instead of staying in all the dull little sandy southern towns of the Carolinas. You would see such pictures. I love your Bermuda sketches a thousand times more than ever now.

I still have that sense of distance which tries one's spirits; but distance is its own cure and remedy, and all but one's swiftest thoughts at last stop flying back, and you get the habit of living where you are. Who was it said that you never get to a place until a day after you come, nor leave it until a day after you go?

(TO MISS LOUISA DRESEL)

Steam Yacht Hermione,
KINGSTON, JAMAICA, *January* 30, 1899.

DEAR LOULIE, — I was so glad to get your letter today, and so was Mrs. Fields. We are having a very much better time as we go on, for A. F. is better and I, too, and I find Jamaica a most enchantingly beautiful country. My fellow travellers say that Ceylon is not a bit more beautiful. We have been a week in Nassau, where I wrote you, and then came down through the Bahamas, stopping only at Inagua, a strange lonely island which I must tell you about some day, with its wild marshes and a huge flock of flamingos, like all your best red paints spilt on the shining mud. There had once been square miles of salt works which were ruined by a tornado, and now the flamingos blow about there like flames. Then we went to Hayti, which was oh, so funny with its pomp of darkeys. Port au Prince was quite an awful scene of thriftlessness and silly pretense — but one or two little Haytian harbours and the high green coast were most lovely. And then Jamaica, with all its new trees and flowers, and its coolies, Loulie! with their bangles and turbans and strange eyes. You would like Jamaica immensely.

Your news of the bicycle is very entertaining. You will be cutting by a slow-footed friend any day after I get back. I think it is so good for you, — one needs a serious reason for getting out of doors sometimes, and a bicycle is a

very serious reason indeed. The roads are so
fine here, winding and looping along the sides
of the hills as they do in Switzerland, — fine
English-made roads, — and you look up to the
great mountains, and down to the blue sea.

I am writing in a hurry to catch a mail, and I
send ever so much love to you and to dear Mrs.
Dresel, and I know A. F. sends her love too.

You will find this an old date, dear Loulie,
but the letter was overlooked when our last
mail was sent ashore, and there has n't been
one since, this being the 19th of February!
We are on our way to Nassau now, expecting
to reach there in a few days. We got into a
port way down in Porto Rico, and after they
had collected all the fees they told us if we
went on to St. Thomas (where all our letters
were!), or to any of the Windward Islands upon
which our hearts were set, we should have to
go through a long quarantine! So we turned
meekly around and came back all our long way,
but we have seen a good many islands and
many rough seas and I feel more resigned
now than I did at first. We are sure to be at
home in two or three weeks now if all goes well.
I think this is a more important postscript
than letter!

Saturday night.

DEAREST, — The letter by Mr. Collyer was from a person who sought to know my opinion of the novel of the future! But he never will.

I copied for him those two wonderful bits of Flaubert, — " Écrire la vie ordinaire comme on écrit l'histoire " ; and the other, " Ce n'est pas de faire rire — mais d'agir a la façon de la nature, c'est à dire de faire rêver." I keep these pinned up on the little drawers at the back of the secretary, for a constant reminder.

I now humbly apologize for presuming to suggest "Wanda," but I thought it would amuse you and waste a day or two's time just as it has done! It grows dull at the last, but it is nice and picturesque at the beginning. I don't believe that you are any the worse for it — you are n't quite equal to hard reading and you must be doing something on account of your grand-mother's having been a May. I hope after this humility to be reinstated in your respect and affection. Novels are good as they go along. It is only when they stop that you take it in that the pretty bubble is made of a spatter of soap suds! (Please to remember this nice simile!)

As you say, what a delightful thing it is to have the mood for books on one and the chance to give up everything for it, but with me it does n't last many days, that enchanting and desperate state of devouring cover and all.

(TO MISS DOROTHY WARD)

SOUTH BERWICK, MAINE, *January* 20, 1900.

MY DEAR DOROTHY, — How good of you to send me this photograph by Sally, who came to bring it one day before I came away from Town! It made me wish to see you the least bit too much, and made me fall at once to thinking how long it is since I saw you in the summer weather at Stocks. But one must look at it often in these sad conditions, and finally gather a good bit of companionship out of a photograph, it being all that one can get! If somebody would only invent a little speaking-attachment to such pictures, a nicer sort of phonograph, — it would really be very nice; you might mention this to your Aunt Ethel with my love. Speaking-likenesses have not really been put into an eager market yet, in spite of the phrase being so old.

I have been wishing to say these many days with what delight we have read the first number of the new story which opened in such a masterful way, and with such large promise. I am hoping for the same windfall which I had when "Sir George" was printing, — of some numbers ahead, — but who knows if such luck will happen to me again? I think the American girl a very living person, the art and the sympathy that went to her writing are most wonderful. I am full of expectation and so is Mrs. Fields; we can hardly say to each other how much we liked that first number and count upon the second, and I have heard many another person say the same. It seems to me like a great success already, but I confess with wistfulness that every time a door opened, I hoped that it was Marcella coming in. *Do not* speak coldly to me of the resources of a great novelist now that you have seen my heart!

Have I owed you a letter for a very long time, dear Dorothy, or is it you who have thought that Sally would give me news and messages? This she has done, but I should

so like a letter to myself from Stocks, with
something about everybody, and even a word
about the pony who brought us safe home,
though such an unwilling person on the road.
I hope that your Mother is just as well as the
story sounds,—and you must give her my
dear love and true thanks. You will both
like to know that Sally is looking very well
this winter— . . . dear child! I have not
seen her half as much as I wish, for I have
been much in the country, and it takes a
good bit more time to live in two places than
in one. Mrs. Fields and I were much tempted
in the autumn to go to Egypt with a friend
who asked us, but I do not like to think of
being so far away from my sister, who would
be very lonely. My nephew is still in Harvard, and we three are all the house now, so
that I have not the heart to take this one
away, and leave but one in the old place. It
is a delightful winter here as to weather, and
yet the shadows and sorrows of war make it
dark enough. The questions of our difficult
Philippines are half forgotten—it is almost
strange to say so—in the anxiety about
South Africa; but I like to take comfort
from this, and other signs, and remember

how much closer Old England and New England have come together in the last two years. That is good, at any rate. I had a most delightful proof of it in the way that many quite unexpected persons felt about a sketch I wrote (and meant to send to you!) called "The Queen's Twin." It was most touching to see how everybody approves it, and told little tales to prove that it might be true — and was at any rate right in its sentiment! But I must not write longer — only to say that I thank you, dear, and that you must not forget to give my love to Jan.

(TO MISS SARA NORTON)

HOTEL BRISTOL, NAPLES, 18 *March*, 1900.

I tell you but short tales of our very stormy and difficult voyage and of water deep in our staterooms and boats going away in the gale, and a beating about in one's berth that I have hardly got over yet, but will go on to say that we have had some good days in Naples and have just come back from two nights at my beloved La Cava with its pigeon towers and reminders of Sir Walter on his last journey. I have been to Pæstum again, which

joy I never expected, and we also had some
hours on Friday at Pompeii. We were going
up to Ravello for a night at least, but it is
quite bitter cold weather just now and has
turned to pouring rain, so that this Sunday
morning we hurried back to our most comfortable quarters here. We still have until
Wednesday, when we start for Brindisi and
Patras. We have had the best of chances to
see the Museum here. There is nothing so
beautiful as this Orpheus and Eurydice, and
I fairly ran to find a certain little Pompeiian
picture of the girl who turns back to gather
flowers! I wonder if you remember it? It is
one of the perfectly un-copyable things. The
spring in Italy seems very cold and late; there
are n't green leaves enough, and everything
has a sort of bony look that makes the really
unlovely things almost unbearable. I caught
myself thinking yesterday as I passed one of
the poorer and newer villages that it was ugly,
and that I could prefer the sight of one of
our own little manufacturing towns with its
quaint rows of sharp gables and even its appar-
ent danger of blowing away! But the grey fig
trees are beginning to show little green silk
tufts, and the olives are quite dark and splendid

on the hills back of Salerno,—as thick and
warm and tufted as one of my own hills of
pines. You see what a New England—I
may say State of Maine—person now holds the
pen! These olives are so much richer than the
olives in Provence where I saw them last: I
can't say how beautiful they were yesterday.

It is a wonderful old Italy though I accuse
it so cheaply of cold and bleakness. Right in
front of me is a flower of asphodel which we
brought from Pæstum yesterday, but the pink
cyclamen were not yet in bloom and very few
daffodils.

(TO MRS. WHITMAN)

ATHENS, 27 *March*, 1900.

Then we came to Brindisi, an all-day journey through green valleys and between great
ranges of the Apennines, all topped with snow,
and took the steamer which got to Corfu
next day and to Greece the next, and then
we were all day again in the trains going along
the southern shore of the Gulf of Corinth,
and at sunset we saw the light on the
Acropolis and all the great pillars of the
Parthenon high against the sky. And pretty

near every waking hour since then I have wished
for you at least once. There is nothing for it
but to go to the Museum every morning, and
to the Acropolis every afternoon.

We make many plots for the next few
weeks. To go to Megara, for instance, to see
the Easter Dances. But oh, how I wish for
you! It is quite true that there is nothing so
beautiful as Athens, the Parthenon and the
marbles in the Museum. I don't suppose that
you have been waiting for me to assure you
of this fact; but when I think what you
would say, and *feel*, at the sight of this
spring landscape and the wintry sky, of such
astonishing blue, with its blinding light, like
one of our winter mornings after a snow-
storm, and the colors of the mountain ranges
and the sea, dazzling and rimmed by far-off
islands and mountains to the south; as one
looks from the Acropolis and all the spring
fields below and the old columns and the little
near-by flowers, poppies and daisies,—Oh,
when I see all this and think that you can't
see it, too! And then, when I remember what
my feelings have been toward the Orpheus
and Eurydice and the Bacchic Dance, and
then see these wonderful marbles here, row

upon row, it is quite too much for a plain
heart to bear. I have come to the place
where I can get quickly through the rooms,
but I must look at a certain *nine* every time
and spend all the time (at present) that I can
get before a special one (or two). If the
special *one* were not next that which has the
young man with his dog, and the old father,
and the little weeping slave - boy, I should
have to divide the aforesaid time into two. It
is n't the least bit of use to try to write about
those marbles, but they are simply the most
human and affecting and beautiful things in
the world. The partings, the promises, are immortal and sacred, they are Life and not only
Lives; and yet the character in them is almost
more than the art to me, being a plain story-
writer, but full of hopes and dreams.

This was a little flower for you that grew
on the Hill today. I feel as if this letter were
too dry and crumpled to send, just as the
flower is, with none of the life of the things
it tries to stand for.

MEGALOPOLIS, 15 *April* [1900].

This is a small town in Arcadia in the
middle of a green plain, to which we came

over the mountains yesterday, driving for the
third, fourth, fifth or sixth day on our journey from the east coast to the west, by Nauplia
and Mycenæ and Epidaurus to Tripolitza and
Sparta. As I write these names, I cannot help
thinking how lately they were nothing but
names; and now each stands for a place unlike any other, and each makes a great landscape rise before one of mountain and plain
and great white columns against the blue sky
and blinding light, and all the Greek flowers
bloom again, asphodels here, and poppies there.

Here in this muddy, noisy little place, we
are opposite the old church with its bell-tower
and single tall cypress, and it is the Greek
Palm Sunday, just a week later than ours.
And all the flocks go tinkling by, and all the
little boys are playing games and squabbling
like sparrows over in the church-yard. But
at home I think of the Class at Easter, and
Katy not there and I not there, and I keep
wondering about you, and if Coolidge will
have come, and I should like to have a flower
in a letter so as to know you thought of me.
I got your dear last letter this week, and heard
about Dr. Mitchell and Owen Wister, and all
those flowering days of mid-March, and I

wish I could pass judgment right now on the portrait. It begins to feel as if we had really come away for a short time, and as if I should be at home again in six weeks if all goes well, but up to this day I have had a queer sense of being off in space, with months before me; of wandering in the East, with dragomen and cooks, and all our bags and shawl-straps to be taken out of the carriage and opened at night, and rolled up and shut again and loaded in the mornings, with a huge new-old stone theatre to see in a hill-side, and the snow mountains looking over the tops of the purple ones in every quarter of Greece. How you would love the handsome sturdy people and the clear-eyed children. Such colors to paint and such glimpses of history in every shepherd on the hills and every hoplite that stalks along the endless roads in his white kilt and stockings and his red cap. Greece is most archaic still to the casual looker-on.

We are just bound down to the coast this afternoon, where we shall take a steamer to the neighborhood of Olympia, and then, if we can get time enough, we go to Delphi before getting back to Athens on the 22d. Then

we mean to go on eastward for a single week
in Constantinople, even if it costs us the sight
of Thessaly; but whether we do the one or
the other is uncertain to me in this present
moment, for sometimes we think of things we
might see in six days to be spent at sea getting back to Venice! But I keep thinking
that I shall never be, so to speak, so handy
to Constantinople again, and I should like to
have the means of making the Arabian Nights
come true. And we shall really have seen so
much of Greece.

I send you much love and many a thought,
and I wish that I could put half the things
into this letter that you would like to read
and I to write. But you must take this leaf
of Bay instead, and call it Palm Sunday or
Easter, just as you like.

(TO MISS SARA NORTON)

MANCHESTER, Tuesday [*June*, 1901].

DEAREST SALLY, — Class day was really an
exquisite thing to see! I did not take in the
beauty of its spectacle until I happened to go
to Dana's room in Holworthy, and to sit on
a window-seat looking down the Yard just be-

fore we went to the Statue. The sun was getting low enough to slant across under the elms, and the lanterns were lit by it before their time with a strange light of day that was better than candles. The people too, though they were going on to the next pleasure, had a look of leisure as they went along the paths, as if they were counting over the last pleasure instead of anticipating a new one. There was such a satisfaction in the beauty of the whole afternoon's festival. I have never seen anything quite like it. I keep thinking as I try to write of that most lovely page of Fitzgerald's in "Euphranor"—"and a nightingale began to sing"—it ends; you remember what I mean?—after the boat-race!

Forgive such a note—my pen will not keep itself steady; it is like trying to write with a small bird's beak!

Yours ever most lovingly.

(TO MRS. FIELDS)

SOUTH BERWICK, Friday afternoon [*June*, 1901].

Here we are at home again. I have so much to tell that my pen splutters. I have had a

beautiful time full of delightful old associations. You can't think how nice it was to be
the single sister of so many brothers at Bowdoin, walking in the procession in cap and
gown and Doctor's hood, and being fetched by
a marshal to the President, to sit on the platform with the Board of Overseers and the
Trustees, also the Chief Justice and all the
judges of the Supreme Court, who were in
session in Portland, or somewhere near by!
And being welcomed by the President in a set
speech as the only daughter of Bowdoin, and
rising humbly to make the best bow she could.
But what was most touching was the old chap-
lain of the day who spoke about father in his
" bidding prayer," and said those things of
him which were all true. And your S. O. J.
applauded twice by so great an audience!

I told Dr. Hyde that I should ask Mrs.
Whitman to make a window. I hope that you
will approve this plan — it will be a really
beautiful and permanent memorial to leave.
They are making up a fund, but the money
that I could give will count so much more in
this way. Mary was dear and lovely, and the
great day was hers as much as mine, as you
will know.

SARAH ORNE JEWETT, LITT. D

From a photograph taken by Miss Elise Tyson in 1903

(TO MISS SARA NORTON)

MANCHESTER BY SEA, *August* 28, 1901.

MY DEAREST SALLY, — I hear of you at Windsor and in other far countries, and the summer goes parading by, here on the shore (where I have been staying once before since August came in), after some perfect days at home, and a bit of a visit to Miss Longfellow at Holderness, where we played much on the lake and in it, and I had one perfectly happy long morning when we went huckleberrying together with enormous profit to the rest of the household! There is a charming sort of easy life going on about those lake shores. One is more shut in by mountains than on Winnipiseogee, — which is so much better known, — and sees all the colours of the great slopes change and change with the slow cloud shadows. The house where I stayed is so close to the lake that the little waves come clucking up to the very walls, and one lands as immediately as if it were Venice, and hears the loons calling as if it were still a wilderness.

My thoughts fly to Stonehurst at this moment and I wonder with considerable wistfulness if we shall really get to that kind house this summer. Perhaps it might be in late September.

"The Tory Lover" got itself quite done at last, — though almost every day I get hurried notes from The House with questions about last things. I grow very melancholy if I fall to thinking of the distance between my poor story and the first dreams of it, but I believe that I have done it just as well as I could. I was delighted the other day when Mrs. Agassiz said that she had been doubtful in the beginning, but had really liked each number better than the last, and I found that my people had made her a real pleasure in the end. One needs these things for cheer.

This morning I have been copying Mr. Kipling's "Bridge-Guard" poem with great delight. Some one lent me his copy cut from the "Times," and I had not succeeded in getting hold of it before. Don't you think it very fine? Don't you feel the same wonderful self-consciousness in it as in "*For to admire and for to see*"? One sees and feels that lonely place in a wonderful way. If you were here how we could talk about it!

On Sunday evening Mrs. Meynell is expected, and both Mrs. Fields and I look forward to seeing her with great pleasure. We have cared a good deal for the thoughtfulness and beauty, and above all for the reticence and restraint, of her poems and brief essays. I suppose that Mr. Ruskin first set our eyes in her direction when he was so enthusiastic long ago about her letter from a girl to her own old age, but it is one of her poems that I really care least about now. One always cares about "Renouncement," that beautiful sonnet, though one discovers after a time that she ought to have called it "Possession," or something of that sort!

It is a great delight that your father has promised to come to dinner on Tuesday. I can't help hoping that I shall see you on Wednesday morning, if not before; Mrs. Meynell has a reading on seventeenth-century poetry. She is going to give it to some club or company in London, and wished to try it here first. It is always interesting (though sometimes a cause for apprehension) to have a friend come in this way — to see an old friend for the first time, as one may say; but both

Shady Hill and 148 Charles Street have gathered many an angel so, and strangers are not real strangers when they are of the world of letters.

I do not forget that we are to see Dorothy again so soon, or to look forward with delight. It is a great pleasure to have had her here in the old house, such guests never really go away — which makes an old house *very* different from a new one !

(TO MR. DAVID DOUGLAS, EDINBURGH)

South Berwick, Maine, *April* 6, 1902.

DEAR MR. DOUGLAS, — The photograph delighted me of the quaint old Scottish house of Traquair ! I had never seen any picture of it. I hope that it may not be many years before my hope comes true of spending some time in Scotland, and seeing many and many an old house. I never forget the pleasure of that day with you both at Hawthornden, how often Mrs. Fields and I speak of it ! You see that I too have run away from town ? It is a very early spring with us. I have never in my life seen our " Mayflowers " (the trailing arbutus) in full bloom on April 6th as I saw them to-day.

(TO MISS SARA NORTON)

SOUTH BERWICK, MAINE, *June* 30 [1902].

I am just having a little visit from Mrs. Riggs, — the author of our beloved "Penelope in Ireland." We have known each other in a pleasant way for a good many years. I happened to be near her in London once, and last week when I happened to be in Brunswick, she was there too, and to my great pleasure said that she should like to come over to Berwick. She *is* the very nice person who wrote our enchanting book. Being with her has reminded me of your pleasure in her story last year, as well as mine. One doesn't always find the writer of the story, — at least in early acquaintance! but with Mrs. Riggs there is the certainty that one might go right on, and see the next chapter, and Salemina and the maid are absent only for the moment.

Great things have been happening in Berwick : there was the 200th anniversary of the old village church (that was the time, 1702, when we were converted by missionaries from Harvard, and before we had been only a little royal colony with Church of England preaching) !

(TO MRS. HARRIET PRESCOTT SPOFFORD)

SOUTH BERWICK, MAINE, *December* 31, 1902.

MY DEAR FRIEND, — I am late in thanking you for my dear little Christmas book, but I wished to read it before I wrote, and these have not been good reading-days. It is a dear story: I felt almost as if I were seven years old again and cuddled into a corner with my beloved story of " Mr. Rutherford's Children." The same feeling came over me as nearly as it ever can come again. Your story walks faster, as a story of these days should, but there are very real people and real experiences, and your charming fancy — your quick imagination — your beloved sympathy, make the pages live. What any " sister authoress " would really love to do would be to hold the pen that was equal to writing *you!*

But I must write no more at this hour of night! I hope to see you very soon, as I am coming back to town presently.

(TO MRS. FIELDS)

Saturday morning.

And now the ball is over, and I suppose a tired hostess, and the chairs all going upstairs

again, and the dear room will look like a green
garden that no wind ever blows over! I do so
long to hear if it went off to your mind, and
if the company liked the singing, and where
it was you hung the lantern! and oh, dear!
a thousand questions!

Yesterday afternoon I amused myself with
Miss Austen's "Persuasion." Dear me, how
like her people are to the people we knew
years ago! It is just as much New England
before the war — that is, in provincial towns
— as it ever was Old England. I am going to
read another, "Persuasion" tasted so good!
I have n't read them for some time.

I long to know if you have read dear Alice
Meynell's paper in the "Atlantic." She has
changed it in places from her lecture to an
essay, and I can't find just the places where
she laughed aloud and all the audience with
her; but what a rich bit of writing it is — and
of such depth and such inexhaustible charm!

Somebody sent me the other day a pamphlet
with an address about Count Rumford, and,
best of all, stuck on a fly-leaf is a cutting
from an old newspaper with the list of their
household goods, which were sold at auction

in Brompton when the countess left London. It mentions *five lofty, four-post beds,* which pleases me much. This was a kind of man who had seen in a newspaper that I was going to write about the Rumfords, and I thank him very much for his pamphlet!

(TO MR. DAVID DOUGLAS, EDINBURGH)

SOUTH BERWICK, MAINE.

DEAR MR. DOUGLAS, — The very day that your letter came I was sending you a copy of Mr. Owen Wister's new story. I find it so delightful — worthy of himself and worthy of Fanny Kemble's journals. It has so charming a humour and so humorous a charm! and tastes as good as the cake itself. The serious talk about the cheap side of American life just now is not at all too severe, but we must look on with what patience we can at the doings of those who have no inherited sense or discretion in the use of money: as a wise old friend said to me not long ago, their grandparents or even their own parents went hungry and ill clothed, and it will take some time for these people to have their fling, to eat all they want and to wear fine raiment, and flaunt authority. They must get to a state, and by slow stages too, where there is going to be something fit for education. "It is just the way that in the South, still, one sees the coloured people on aimless journeys: in the old days they could not leave their plantations. They won't be satisfied with that exercise of liberty for generations yet!" The years of leanness are succeeded by many more than seven fat years in all these people. The trouble is to us old-fashioned New Englanders that 'the cheap streak' so often spoils what there is of good inheritance, and the wrong side of our great material prosperity is seen almost everywhere. These are sad reflections! —but I often remind myself of the better side of life, a hope that it is truly an immortal sort of leaven.

My Lockhart came to-day and, as I had expected, I found you before I had gone far in the preface. Do not write just to acknowledge the book; those dutiful notes rob us of time to write the letters we care more for!

Our "Atlantic" editor, Mr. Bliss Perry, goes over to England this summer. I hope you will see him in Edinburgh, — a delightful man with true enthusiasm for the best things.

I have been hoping to write to you, but,
oddly enough now, when I am supposed to be
better, it has grown a great deal harder either
to read or write. But I shall not let you go
away without a word to say how much I love
you. I am glad you liked that little book of
Mrs. Meynell's. There is something so charming to me in the way she arranged it — the
harmony — and the inevitableness of her own
choice and good taste have done that perhaps.
I had a little hope that you might carry it with
you; sometimes it has been the only book that
I could read for days. I was so sorry that I
sent it away with such smudgy fly-leaves, —
you might take an idle day on shipboard and
make it clean again! I have a bad habit of
writing in my books as if no one else were
ever going to read them.

This year she wrote in the spring to her
friend Ellen Chase: —

" Did you hear all the song-sparrows as
they came by on their way to Berwick?

" I have been ill, but you will tell me if the

'Pointed Firs' look all right this year, won't you?"

(TO MRS. HENRY PARKMAN)

MANCHESTER BY SEA, Wednesday.

DEAREST FRANCES, — Did you ever see a little sermon called "Happiness," that S. W. wrote years ago, and printed in a book that Mrs. James Lodge put together? partly her own writing, with a really delightful preface, and partly stories — translations and verses, etc.; all amateur work in a way, but it made a pretty gold and white book called "A Week away from Time." I had much to do with it and it always brings back some very pleasant things. Mrs. Fields and I re-read the sermon on Sunday, after I had again got hold of it myself, and with new admiration. Mrs. Fields always said that it was the best of the book and liked it dearly, but I was not so sure *then*, and on Sunday I liked it a thousand times more than ever before. I'll send you the book if you like and *don't* know it.

I had a most dear letter from Mrs. Wolcott. I wish that you and she could read "The Way it Came," my favorite among all Mr. James's stories, together, when she gets to you. I marked that, and "The Liar," which comes next, in their respective volumes. "The Way it Came" is a *great* story, *I* think, so full of feeling and of a subtle knowledge of human nature, of the joyful hopes, and enlightenments and grey disappointments of life — the things we truly *live* by! — I don't know how many times I have read this or the half dozen others that come next: "The Liar," "The Death of the Lion," etc.

POLAND SPRING HOUSE, Monday.

I think this great place would amuse you some time — perhaps we could forsake the world together for a week! — but the line between being innocently amused and wickedly bored is very narrow. It is a little like what crossing the continent with a big train party must be, — not the people you or I run across very often, but all sorts of terrible rich and splendid westerners and southerners of a sort who must have had German grand-mas and have prospered in the immediate past. Their jewels and their gowns are a wonder, and the satisfaction in life must be very great, though the best of them look as if keeping things just right and *according to* at this high rate were almost too much effort. It is the kind of rich creatures who are more at home in big hotels than in fine houses. They are apt to speak of last winter at " Pa'm Beach," and altogether they made me understand what my old grand-father, who had travelled wide, meant when he said, " Oh, they 're not people, they 're nothing but a pack of images ! " This is in the mass ; one individual opposite me at the table has been quite entertaining ; such a diamond cross she wears upon her ; but I must hold back from relating such parts of her history as have been ascertained, — automobile and private car. A great many puzzling facts were brought together into simple certainty yesterday when I heard somebody say she was a prosperous retired hotel-keeper. It made you see her fine and masterful above quailing maids. These dazzle one's eyes; but now and then, when you see the backs of two dear heads of ladies a table or two away, you feel as if you must stop and speak ! I feel sure out of two or three hundred fellow pilgrims I must find as many of my betters, but I have been so long away that my country seems strange in its great crowd of citizens. One thing certain is, it is a rich country, — it is like Rome before it fell ! And the clouds have all blown out of the mountains yesterday and today. I can see them all safe and sound,—the Mount Washington range just as I used to see it all last summer; but we are far enough away to see the other ranges by themselves — Ossipee and the rest.

(TO MISS SARA NORTON)

Thursday, *November* 20.

How much I wish for you at this moment, Sally dear! but it must be a heavenly day at Newport, and without this touch of the North that makes a fire not look unwelcome in my room. Now that the leaves are down I can see the smooth top of my hill like a little Yorkshire moor, and it makes me wish that we were walking there again. Oddly enough I am just reading one of Mrs. Ritchie's stories that keeps one much out of doors in the Lake Country, — "Mrs. Dymond,"— and between reading and looking up at the hill, I got too keen a sense of being housebound! One flies to Miss Thackeray's stories at certain turns of Fate, for a world full of shadows, and written out of deep and touching experience, but with beauty and consolation never forgotten or cur-

tained away. Don't you remember Fitzgerald's
saying somewhere that he thirsts for the Delightful as he grows old and dry? Perhaps
he was writing about Miss Thackeray then —
the Village on the Cliff which he really loved.

Get rested, dear, and make the most of
these days in Newport by doing just the least
you can with them! I think of you most lovingly and oftener than I can dare to say. As
for me, I am much the same, getting back little
by little to ordinary life, but not downstairs
yet, or equal to much that can be really called
decent or properly useful behaviour.

(TO MISS ELLEN CHASE)

SOUTH BERWICK, MAINE,
Friday, 23 *September*, 1904.

MY DEAR ELLEN, — I must thank you, too,
for your royal present of the Herbal, which
was waiting for me when I got home from the
mountains. I am put on such short commons
of reading and writing, and can manage to do
so little of either, yet, that after the first delighted look I had to fall back on the (after
all!) deep joys of possession. But I look forward to the day when I can quite live between

the covers of that great book. I have thought
of you many and many a time this summer,
and always with a true gratitude for your
dear thoughtfulness and kindness in so many
ways.

Yours most affectionately.

(TO CHARLES MINER THOMPSON)

SOUTH BERWICK, MAINE,
October 12, 1904.

MY DEAR MR. THOMPSON, — I wish that
I could have written sooner to tell you how
deeply I feel the kindness and sympathy for
my stories in your "Atlantic" paper. Perhaps you may know already that I have not
yet recovered from a bad accident and long
illness that followed it, and that I find it very
difficult now to read or to write, and so you
will not have thought me unmindful of such
friendliness as you have shown to me and to
my work. If you felt the difficulty of which
you speak in your first paragraph, in writing
about a writer, I feel, too, as one might who
heard some one begin to speak frankly of one's
self in the next room. This has been an innocent
sort of eaves-dropping, and not without profit

and suggestion, as well as happy reassurance
for me. Indeed, I understand that "The
Country Doctor" is of no value as a novel, but
it has many excellent ideas, for which I must
thank not only my father's teaching, but my
father himself. It only makes me wish to see
you some day, when we can talk together as
much as we wish, now that I am trying to
write this letter to you; indeed, there are many
points in your paper that give one something
to think about and to say. I was looking at
a translation of one of Turguenieff's stories,
"Rudin," not long ago, and came upon something in Stepniak's preface to the book which
struck me deeply with its likeness to some of
your own words about — not a Master by any
means, but a story-writer of certain instincts!
"But there was in him such a love of light,
sunshine, and living human poetry, such an or-
ganic aversion to all that is ugly, or coarse, or
discordant, that he made himself almost exclu-
sively the poet of the gentler side of human nature. On the fringe of his pictures, or in their
background, just for the sake of contrast, he will
show us the vices, the cruelties, even the mire
of life. But he cannot stay in these gloomy
regions, and he hastens back to the realms of

the sun and the flowers, or to the poetical
moonlight of melancholy, which he loves best
because in it he can find expression for his
own great sorrowing heart."

I find myself copying the whole of this, —
but you would like the whole preface: it is in an
edition lately republished here by Macmillan,
edited by Mr. Garnett. I did not know much
of Turguenieff in earlier years, but there is
all the greater pleasure in making one's self
familiar now with all his work. I remember
Mr. Howells asking me with great interest long
ago when I had written the story of a "Land-
less Farmer," if I knew Turguenieff's "Lear
of the Steppe"; but I did not then or for a
few years after. I confessed to Mr. Perry that
I never was a Hawthorne lover in early life!
I am afraid now that it was a dangerous
admission to have made to my kind essayist
editor! but I tell this also to you, since after
what you said, it will not be without interest;
we come to our work by strange paths — we
hardly know how. It was hard for this person (made of Berwick dust) to think of herself as a "summer visitor," but I quite understand your point of view; one may be away from
one's neighborhood long enough to see it quite

or almost from the outside, though as I make this concession I remember that it was hardly true at the time of "Deephaven."

I must not try to write longer, but I shall be looking forward to seeing you. I hope that this may be when winter comes, for I hope to be well enough then to get to town. I can seldom think at all about the affairs of writing, of which my mind used always to be full. Once lately something made me turn to one of my stories — "The Only Rose"; I read it to a young friend who wished to hear it, with a very strange feeling, because there it was, quite alive and well, even if its writer was no longer good for any writing at all. You will see by this what pleasure I could get from your serious and interested talk about all the stories; I liked to think that they were so alive to some one, and had given, or could still give pleasure.

Believe me, with my best thanks and regards to so kind a friend,

Yours most sincerely,

S. O. JEWETT.

SOUTH BERWICK, Thursday,
November 3, 1904.

MY DEAR LOUISA, — If you knew how much
pleasure your note and the exquisite photograph gave me yesterday, you would never
forbid my writing a word to say so! I only
wish you would come flying down like one of
your own pigeons, out of the blue sky, so that
we could talk as much as we wish about the
Hermes. I find in the note that you felt there
at Olympia just as I felt! The *light on the
face* in this photograph is nearest the real
thing of any picture or copy of any sort whatever that I know.

Thank dear K. for her last note. I hope to
see you both before winter gets very far, but
my last grind of " headaches " and " the pre-
vailing fall cold " on top of it have sent this
slow patient down hill again. Never mind!
there ought to be time enough for everything,
taking this world and the next together !

Yours lovingly.

SOUTH BERWICK, MAINE,
December 14, 1904.

MY VERY DEAR FRIEND, — I have been thanking you in my heart all this time for the letter which came in the summer, just when I was most grateful for such pleasure of getting hold of your hand again. The letter and the beautiful Cowper preface came together: I was in retreat at the Mountains, staying alone in a journeying - friend's big country house with my nurse for many weeks, — the doctors had forbidden both writing and reading; but on a long day it happened that by an odd chance, *this* letter of all letters, being forwarded with other things, dropped into my hands! I *had* to read it and read it and hold it fast to my heart, — the nurse looking on with true sympathy. One of the first things when she came, a stranger, and we were a little uncertain of each other's claws (!) I was fretting because I hadn't brought at least two or three books that I loved. I wished for your poems and almost cried as I said so. — "I've got that book in my trunk!" said dear Miss O'Bryan with shining face, and we feared each

other's claws no more! She used to read to me
a little now and then; I never knew how I
loved you, either in your work or out of it, before that summer brought me a long way further into the country of our friendship. It is
very strange to go through this long time of
silence; a strange loss of balance followed the
terrible blow on my head, and I am not yet
free from its troubles or from the attacks of
pain in the back of my head. People say,
"Can't you write a little?" but in nothing
can that sense of balance count as it must in
writing. I am stronger, I am even going to
town presently. I am so often thinking of you
in the long hours when I crochet instead of
reading everything as one used! I do read a
little every morning now, in Santa Teresa's
Letters,— and I pick up other things now and
then for a little while, but my wits get blurred
over, easily. Say that you and Mr. Meynell
are coming over in the spring, when you write
again! And take all my heart's wishes for a
happy Christmas for you and for those you
love, dear.

(TO MISS DOROTHY WARD)

South Berwick, Maine,
December 14, 1904.

My dearest Dorothy, — I have been looking through our dear Mrs. Whitman's letters
to me, — of many years, — much beloved letters! and this morning I happened to find one
of yours which had strayed among them. You
can hardly think with what true pleasure and
delight I have read it, — a letter written just
after you had left Levens. You will remember
the afternoon on Cartmell Fell, of which you
and Sally both told me; I wish that I could
find *her* letter too, for I love to go back to it
all.

You should be here now, so that we might
talk about that day and many other days. I
wish very much to hear from you and to know
what you are doing, as I did know then,
dear. It is a very long time since I have
seen Sally, — not since one afternoon last May,
which I dearly love to remember because I
believe she was never closer to one's heart.
This long pull of illness makes one feel a
little like being dead! — for many months I
could not read or write, and even now I find

neither very easy; but things are mending
slowly, and this week I am making the great
adventure of going to Town for a little while.
The temptations of Town are much greater
than the temptations of dear Berwick, but it
is good to have the change I am sure. And I
shall see Sally just as soon as I can and tell
you about her. Everybody is reading William
Ashe and Lady Kitty as if they were alive and
behaving nobly and excitingly before one's
very eyes. The story is quite splendidly talked
about even here in little old Berwick, and
there is that pain when the new "number" is
read and there must be a whole month's waiting for another one, which is the highest trib-
ute to a great novelist. In the summer I was
a long time in getting a "number" read, —
by little pieces with sometimes days between,
— and that taught me its quality, I can tell
you. Please give my love, and my pride, too!
to your Mother. I feel sometimes as if nobody
knew as well as I what a noble piece of work
she can do! Perhaps this is n't true, but nobody takes greater pleasure or pride.

Yours ever lovingly.

(TO MRS. FIELDS)

June 25, 1905.

Here is another rainy Monday, much no-
ticed in housekeeping. Yesterday was such
a lovely day, and the strange thing to me was
to remember how exactly the weather was like
it last year, — the Sunday morning when I
heard that dear S. W. had gone. I remember
well that long bright day and the wonderful
cloud I watched at evening floating slowly
through the upper sky on some high current
northward, catching the sun still when we
were in shadows. I could not help the strange
feeling that it had something to do with her.
It was like a great golden ball or balloon, as
if it wrapped a golden treasure; her golden
string (that Blake writes about) might have
made it. Those days seem strangely near.
After a whole year one begins to take them
in.

(TO MRS. PARKMAN)

SOUTH BERWICK, Monday afternoon, 1905.

MY DEAREST FRANCES, — I now state (but
with a strange pen found on Mary's desk)
that "*Please send 2d Revise to*" is the form

of words, and after a bad night and day made
doubly trying by little problems about these
dear proofs.[1] I begin to cheer up because you
say that you will come on Thursday. We feel
sadly provincial since the fast expresses have
made a new schedule and go right by, but
there is a *nice* 1.15 train to Dover where I
could meet you, and if you can stay long
enough, you can go to York by trolley (this
bait has been used before without being no-
ticed by Frances).

I just opened an October "Spectator" that
I had not seen, and here in a Review of
the Queen's Letters some wise person says:
"We realize of course that it is exceedingly
difficult to print Documents or Letters entire
owing to reasons of space. *At the same time
it cannot be doubted that a letter is a living thing with an individuality of its own,
and if the head and tail are cut off, and two
or three pieces taken out of the body, that
individuality is lost.*" This is my own strong
instinct. I have felt Her at my elbow so often
in reading these proofs that it has been hard
not to follow *our* dislikes or preferences, but
I would not for anything be *prepotente.* I

[1] Mrs. Whitman's Letters.

think we should think of the author first however in every case. That's our plain duty.

But so few of us know what a stern judge *print* is in itself; what a sifter and weigher of values, how astonishing its calm verdict when a book is *done*. None of these preliminary stages can forecast it, and I do so want this to be Her best. What she would wish it. Too much choosing has cost the letters dear; they sometimes do not read like letters at all in these unrelated fragments. I cannot keep myself from thinking how beautiful she made them, each was like one of her own sketches. She brought all her Art to letter writing when she was at her best. She would say we must make them stand as well as we can. . . .

This is only said to *you* by your loving
S. O. J.

(TO MRS. WHEELWRIGHT)

MANCHESTER BY SEA,
Wednesday, *7th August.*

It is not because I do not think of you very often that I have not written; but every day brings its succession of little hurries, and hours when one cannot write. And then I count

more and more upon the truth that we can
"think" to each other, when we are really
friends, much better and oftener than we can
write. When they find out all about wireless
telegraphy, they are going to find out how
the little batteries in our heads send messages,
and then we can do it by rule and not by accident. It is very nice now, however, and we
are n't *called up* by strangers as we may be in
those later and more instructive days. You see
that I am here, alone with Mrs. Fields, just
now, though we had two young men for Sunday, Mr. Woodberry and Mr. Greenslet (who
wrote Mr. Lowell's life last year), and there
was no end of talk about book affairs and especially about Sicily, — Taormina, — where they
had all three been. I listened as if I had been
there too, having read them — and others.
Mrs. Fields had six weeks at Taormina three
years ago, and I know her point of view lit-
erally and figuratively both.

You have had a new sorrow in these days
— it has been in my mind all the time I have
been writing. I have had a feeling that it would
touch you closely. It is hard to have people
go when they take a piece of our lives with
them. I have sometimes felt as if it were I

who died and stopped, and not they. " They
are all gone into a world of light," as
Vaughan says (oh, that most beautiful poem !),
but it leaves it darker here.

I have just been sitting and thinking about
you with my pen in my hand. I wish that I
were nearer to you. We could be out in the
" Solace," and yet we need n't try to talk.

(TO MRS. FIELDS)

Yesterday I went to church and heard Dr.
Lewis's sermon about the Queen, which was
very well done, and there was a display of
the English flags about a big picture of the
Queen, and two wreaths of Berwick evergreens,
tied with black! I have lived so much this
last year in thought of the days when there
was bitterest feeling toward England, that the
sight of these things in the old meeting house
astonished me more than it could have astonished anybody else in the congregation ; but
it was a most pleasing sight. There are some
English parishioners, mill people; I suppose
the portrait — a big engraving of some sort
— came in that way. I saw tears in many eyes,
however ; the sermon was very touching, but

the whole feeling was as if some kind person had died in our own little neighbourhood.

Monday morning — and what do you think is on this day but little Miss Grant's funeral, the poor soul having got through at last and suddenly. So Mary and I are going down to Portsmouth to the service, which is to be in the little hospital. I can't take it in that I shall see that lively, friendly, quaint, busy creature no more. My stories are full of her here and there, as you know, and she has made a great part in the rustic side of my life and so in the town side. Well, it is one of the moments when I am glad to think that there shall not be any more tears, neither sorrow nor sighing.

Thursday noon.

I have finished "Ivanhoe" and also a story of Ouida's which is called "A Village Commune" — a most powerful, harrowing story of the wrongs put by greedy officials on the Italian peasants. There is not a trace of her vulgarity in this; it is as powerful a story, and strikes as straight at wrong-doing as Tolstoi's best — with all the knowledge of human nature and a lovely descriptive gift thrown in. Ouida is a great writer — when she is at her

best, there is no getting over that fact. If she
did n't lose her head, and — perhaps — were
she not a woman, we should hear much more
of Ouida! particularly of her " Village Commune."

Katie just brought up the " Herald," which
comes earlier than the Post-office things, and
I see that Owen Wister has been Telling the
Truth! Hurrah! for they see what the matter is, when all sorts of facts are being expen-
sively crammed into boys' and girls' minds
without making those minds grow, or enlarging
the thoughts of the individual. I think the pro-
cesses of exams. are at the bottom. There is
something out of gear about graded schools
and all that. Memory is developed at the ex-
pense of what in general we are pleased to
call thought and character.

Monday.

I wish to tell you one thing, dear, that I
knew Lieutenant Wallingford was killed, none
better, but how could I write about him unless I kept him alive? — There is something
so strange now, that I can hardly believe it
myself. I thought about him and his house

and the members of the family whom I have
known, and made him a Tory and had Mary
W—— challenge him to his duty, all out of
my own imagination; and on Saturday I got
a package of notes from Mr. Buell in which it
is proved that Wallingford was a Tory and
his lady love declined to marry him for that
reason; at last he took her challenge and went
to sea. He confessed to Paul Jones that he
had come for a lady's sake and not from his
principles. Part of this is told almost in my
words of the story, as you shall see. Now how
could I have guessed at his character, and what
was likely to happen, and better? Imagination
is the only true thing in the world!

Yesterday I took up an old volume of
Scott's "Lives of the Novelists," and read the
brief sketches of Horace Walpole and Dr.
Johnson and Goldsmith with great delight.
He did them so lightly — with such ease and
good sense. How one admires that great man
more and more! I must tell you that in
a book of short essays of Edmund Gosse's
that Louise Guiney gave me last Christmas,
I found a very nice paper about Edward
Fitzgerald. I always love that bit about his
having been reading and lazily sitting in his

garden idly to watch things grow, "for *which I think I shall be damned!*" as he complacently adds.

Monday morning.

I had a really beautiful day yesterday. I stayed at home from church in the morning and took up President Eliot's life of his son, and I don't know when anything has moved me so much. You remember how beautiful the magazine paper was that President Eliot wrote about one of their island neighbours down at Mount Desert—and this is written with that same veracity and Defoe-like closeness to the fact, and with such deep affection as one seldom feels in a book. I finished it last night, for although it is a big volume, much of the latter half preserves his own reports of work on the Metropolitan Park Commission, etc., which one does not need to know exactly, at least in the first reading, though this will interest you deeply. So I am sending it right over to you.

The dining-room looks as it used now, and is so much pleasanter! but when we had all the birds, the cardinal, and the charming sparrows, and all those, they were really very nice. I don't care much for any of these, especially since I came home this last time to find that dear bright wise little Bobby, father's tame little bird that he was so fond of, was dead and gone. There never was a little creature with so true and good a heart. He knew so many things—though not one trick! and he would chirp at me until I answered and spoke to him, and then would sing himself to pieces. How often I have laughed and begged him to be still; and now that live little voice is . still enough and its wisp of grey feathers. John and I put him into a little box, and buried him when nobody else knew it, down under the grass on father's grave, where so much sweet cheerfulness lies still already. It was one of the dear links with those old days, you know, dear, and I can't help thinking that Bobby's spark of life is not put out altogether.

Tuesday morning.

What do you think I am reading but "Middlemarch," though I confess that I have to make skips often. How much more she dwells and harps than in "Adam Bede" and "Silas Marner." She draws her characters so that they stand alive before you, and you know what they have in their pockets, and then goes on for three pages analyzing them and their motives; but after all one must read them with patience for the sake of occasional golden sentences, that have the exactness and inevitableness of proverbs. Perhaps I read my "Middlemarch" too late in the evening, but I find very dull stretches in it now and then. But think of Mr. Casaubon being but forty-five at the time of his marriage! I think of him as nearly seventy and old for his years at that, and indeed he must have been growing old since he was born, and never have had a season of merely ripening. It is a wonderfully drawn character to me, the pathos and reality of it. How I should like to go on talking about it.

What do you think I am reading with deepest interest but Mahan's "Influence of Sea Power on History," which is perfectly delightful! I don't know whether you would care much about it, though it is not too technical and nautical, but rather historical. One thing is so nice, about the fleets that are attacked having the best chance (according to the French). They stay in their places while the enemy comes at them, but wastes power in coming, and then, the principle holding good from the days of galleys until now, the attacked fleet has kept its power in reserve and its men fresh to resist. You get so interested before you know it. I have been interested in what I saw about the book for a long time, and I find it a great pleasure to have it. The use of English words is so fresh and good and the whole tone so manly and sailor-like.

Well, I must n't write about folkses this busy morning, but tell important tales about my walking up the garden yesterday afternoon, and hearing a great buzz-buzzing over among the apple trees, and seeing the whole air brown with a swarm of bees, and rushing for one of the old hives and trying to take them; but off they went, leaving part of their company about some comb which they had fastened on a bough of a tree, a thing I never saw before. Minnie, who is an experienced country person from Bantry Bay, as we have long known, came out ringing a bell as if she were one of those who took the bees in that pretty "Georgic" of Virgil. There never was anything simpler or prettier. We got the remainder bees and their pieces of white new comb into the hive, and there they are, I suppose, in all the rain. I coveted the big swarm that went away. It was such a pretty, lucky thing to go out and find them.

(TO MISS SARA NORTON)

SOUTH BERWICK,
Monday, *March* 26 [1906].

DEAREST SALLY,—Today is town-meeting day and I am sitting by Mrs. Fields's desk at the front window (it has to move from the window where you knew it in winter), and it is very funny, beside giving rise to thoughts, to see the farmers and their country sleighs and their wives who come " trading " ! You may have seen an Ashfield town-meeting, but our eastward region about Agamenticus " Mountain," between us and the sea, is still in a very old-fashioned state of mind—its expression in the men's dress is like early " Biglow Papers " times—fur caps made from what must be long extinct animals, but good common-sense rules the rulers for the most part; and I should like to shake hands hard with two or three of them, and they would say, " Now which one o' the Doctor's *girls* be you ! " This is a nice

neighbourhood: I wish that you (and I) knew
it better.

(TO MRS. WHEELWRIGHT)

Sunday, at Mrs. Cabot's,
PRIDE'S CROSSING [1906].

MY DEAR SARAH, — I think of you and of
writing to you every day, but it does not seem
to have been good writing weather! I have
been thinking as much of my days with you
and with Frances, too, as of what I have been
doing since. If there is a good wind I say to
myself that we can go sailing in the "Hes-
per." No matter if I am land-locked, I go on
living with you as if I had never come away.

I came here in time to see the Watteau fête,
and felt as if Isabel quite belonged to me!
She was *delightful* in her part, and made a
centre for the gay little crowd of players. The
prettiest thing besides that was the classic
touch: beside this foreground of gay French
gentry there was a little group in the green
field behind, at the edge of the sea, of a shepherd with his pipe, a nymph who danced de-
lightfully, and the small heathen god Eros,
with his bow and arrows and a garment of
leopard skin and green chaplet for his young

sunburnt head, with a sheep and a lamb that followed him when he followed the happy pair. The dance was charming, but at the close, when shepherd and nymph strayed away down the field to the sea and Eros strayed after, and the sheep and lamb after him, it made a live little procession that came right from a page of Theocritus! I would give anything if you three had seen it with me. I should like to see the players among the blue-bells on your green turf at Sutton's Island — the place was made for such as they.

I found the old address of my father and sent it to Mr. Wheelwright, but he must not vex himself by reading it — if it does not appeal. I was only interested to find how much my father had anticipated of the condition of things now in " practice," and especially the contempt of remedies, with which I have but little patience. It seems as if there *were* such a thing as Therapeutics, and as if it were just as ignorant to take too little medicine as to take too much.

PRIDE'S CROSSING, Sunday, *August* 5 [1906].

I am ending my summer visit to Mrs. Cabot
on Wednesday, when I go to Mrs. Fields, and
Miss Ellen Emerson is to be there on Wednesday, too. I have really come back to some sense
of pleasure in life ; though I feel like a dis-
sected map with a few pieces gone, the rest of
me seems to be put together right! There are
a great many delightful people to see, and I
always delight in my visit here — each one is
a treasure as it comes, and this was one of the
perfect Sunday mornings when my dear old
friend and I sat alone together and felt very
near each other's heart. I must tell you what
we read with great delight — the life of Miss
Catharine Sedgwick! We each passed it to the
other to read some delightful page, and 'the
other' would read on in silence until a craving
for sympathy made her unselfish enough to
pass it back again. I did not know how good it
was. I fancied it had been written in the dull
time of " Memoirs," but I was quite wrong;
it was just as well to wait and grow a good
deal older before I went back to it, and Mrs.

Cabot had not opened it for many years. It is a charming picture of my mother's and your grand-mother's New England. Mrs. Kemble's letter at the end is one to learn by heart. There is a page, too, about the advantages of country life, that made me "fire up" about Berwick as I used in my best days! There is another pleasure in being here. I often see Miss Caroline King, who was one of your Uncle James Lowell's early friends; she talks about him more and more as she grows older, and yesterday, when I went to see her just at the other end of this short beach, she lent me a tiny volume of Shakespeare sonnets that he gave her in the early forties, with all his marks and bits of notes and a quotation from "Bussy d'Ambois" on the fly-leaf — all her youth and his are shut like a little flower between the small covers — it is a dear little book! I have seen it before, but yesterday she lent it, and touched it as if it were a flower still in bloom. They knew how to read poetry, that company of friends — their hearts were full of it.

MY DEAR ELLEN,—I should like to have a word from you to know if you are well and not minding these huge heaps of snow! I left Berwick as brown as a squirrel on all the hills, and came back to find it very white with snow. I wished to send a note to you to ask you to come in while I was in town; but I was very unequal to things most of the time, and the good days when I dared to plan for a little more than the day was going to bring, were sadly few. Next time I hope to be more free, but when I have bad days with the pain in my head it makes so much trouble for other people.

Do you feed the winter birds, and are there many of those hungry little companies this year? I don't see anybody but sparrows, and they seem to take such excellent care of themselves, — one does have one's favorites among all two-footed beings!

I felt very much your kind sympathy at the time of my aunt's death. She is one to be most sadly missed — the last of my three dear grand-aunts, and they all died last year, and now their houses must all be shut, — dear and beautiful and full of kindness ever since I can remember. I often say this to myself with a thankful heart. It was wonderful to have kept them all so long.

(TO MRS. WHEELWRIGHT)

SOUTH BERWICK, MAINE,
Monday, 7*th May*, 1907.

DEAR SARAH WHEELWRIGHT, — I meant to write you sooner, but last week, between, 1st, a cold going off, and 2d, a journey coming on, I was not good for much. I believe no longer in Habit, for why should writing be the most difficult thing now when I spent all my life once in doing it? Let us not discuss these things! I have had such pleasure all the week in remembering last Sunday afternoon, and "the shrubbery" makes a background for many unrelated figures of this foreground. You gave me a great deal more pleasure than you knew in making that kind little plot. I thank my Club for its kind welcome, and I wish that I could appear on the 12th, but, as you thought, it won't do just now. I am not good for much, but what can be done must be done here — things are coming right up in the

garden. I won't say that I can't leave home when
the old asparagus-bed is in its early prime, because you might think that quite low; but the
poplars must also be trimmed where the ice-
storm broke them in March — *you* know how
many little reasons go to making up big ones,
and I have really been away a great deal lately
from this dear old house, so that my sister and
I plan many things together. I belong to the
Club all the same, and I am sorry not to say
yes when you ask me to do anything, having
a deep sense of a true belongingness of friendship. It has been something very dear and
happy in these late winter and spring days.

How charming all this is about your neighbours! the true and "simple life," full of such
beautiful "lines" as you artists would say,
genuineness and power of enjoyment; as I
write this I wonder if a certain state of mind
that we call power of enjoyment didn't go out
of fashion when the old feeling of worship did
in going to church. Life became such a matter of opinions then; but this is beyond me to
write about. Most persons go round it in a
circle and come back to saying that it is a
matter of temperament; but the garden isn't
a matter of temperament, — it is an old plot

of ground where several generations have been trying to make good things grow.

The sun must be shining in at your windows beautifully today. Do go to Lincoln, that's the proper way to cope with busy gentlemen. Berwick and Lincoln are both better than *down town*. Good-bye; I send you both my love.

(TO MR. GEORGE E. WOODBERRY)

SOUTH BERWICK, MAINE, 23d *August*, 1907.

DEAR MR. WOODBERRY, — Your letter found me here. — I meant for you to keep the two little books. I am sure that you will care enough for them — for reason of " Renouncement" in one volume and " My Lady Poverty" in the other, if for nothing else! What a picture of Italy that last brief poem never fails to make before one's eyes! I wish that we could talk about them while they are still fresh in your mind.

What a joyful time it is to be close to the end of a long piece of work, and sad too — like coming into harbour at the end of a voyage. The more one has cared to put one's very best into a thing, the surer he is to think that it falls far short of the "sky he meant." But it is certain that everything *is* in such work that we have put in. The sense of failure that weighs the artist down is often nothing but a sense of fatigue. I always think that the trees look tired in autumn when their fruit has dropped, but I shall remember as long as I remember anything a small seedling apple tree that stood by a wall in a high wild pasture at the White Hills, — standing proudly over its first small crop of yellow apples all fallen into a little almost hollow of the soft turf below. I could look over its head, and it would have been a heart of stone that did not beat fast with sympathy. There was Success! — but up there against the sky the wistfulness of later crops was yet to come.

(TO MISS SARA NORTON)

SOUTH BERWICK, MAINE, *November* 12, 1907.

MY DEAREST SALLY, — I have just tied up a little book for you. It may not 'like you' as much as the "Hortus Vitæ," but I find many charming things in it. I suppose that I am made like Vernon Lee; it gave me a little thrill the other day when I came upon this in still another book called "Limbo": "As some persons are never unattended by a melody, so others — and among them your humble servant — have always for their thoughts and feelings an additional background besides the one which happens to be visible behind their head and shoulders." — I must lend you "Limbo" some day, or find it for you. I always fancy that you may like, even better than I (because you are a closer friend), to have these brief sketches open their windows toward Italy.

I ought not to write on and on to a busy autumn Sally in this way, but the thing I really had most in mind when I began was the story of an Indian summer afternoon last week, when I went on a little pilgrimage by trolley car down the Kittery shore, to a dear old house on the river just opposite Portsmouth, where my sister and I used to visit a delightful old grand-aunt — by courtesy and *of* courtesy — when we were children. You go down a deep lane from the main road and (I ought to tell this to Dr. James) I was possessed by a sudden terror of a huge Newfoundland puppy who used to run and jump at me when I was six years old. I never have been so afraid of anything since. I was not thinking of him after a comparative safety of above fifty years. There's a persistent sensation for you! The old house was standing empty and somebody let us in to stay as long as we liked. It is a huge old place, I can't quite remember all the rooms now! and the sun was shining in, and the dear ghosts : Aunt Anne and Cousin Marcia were both there. It is far too long to write after all, but the sound of Portsmouth bells across the water woke many things in my heart. And in the old garden, as if Aunt Anne would even now not let us go empty-handed away, there was the last old St. Michael's pear-tree that I know, with its harvest dropped for us on the grass. I wrote a story about this old house once, called "Lady Ferry," — it was when I was about twenty and still very young, and Mr. Howells would not print it. I can always show him the scar to his great amusement! I put it into my second small book, "Old Friends and New," and you might just look at it ; I still think that he made a mistake (I can hear him laugh!), but it was my whole childish heart written in. I have only seen dear Mr. Howells two or three times all summer. They were just going away when Mrs. Fields was here, when he

generally comes up for an afternoon or so.
He looks very well, I think much better than a
year ago or two. Was not his "Atlantic" paper
full of kind and delightful things, and Mr.
Norton's so exactly right! and Miss Francis's
in the last "Contributors' Club" about Mr.
Fields; those were the days when I began!

Dear Sally, forgive all this, but I have
been playing that I really saw you and your
dear father. The trouble is that you have not
known it and told me instead the things that
I would so much rather hear. I am sure that
you were both glad to get back to Shady
Hill, and I hope that you are both equal to
many pleasures and to the things you wish to
do. You and Mr. Norton are two of my very
dearest little company of friends; I can
never help thinking of you both very often
and always sending my true love.

(TO MISS ELIZABETH McCRACKEN)

148 Charles Street, BOSTON, *December* 28.

MY DEAR MISS McCRACKEN, —My last
copy of your delightful book was just going
to my friend Madame Blanc-Bentzon in Paris
when you put this one into my hand! — You

see that I have — unconsciously, too ! — been
behaving with it as some one else did with
a certain book called "The Country of the
Pointed Firs"! And this I shall keep, with a
great pleasure of thankfulness in remembering your kind thought of me. I wish to say
what an excellent piece of work I believe
"The Women of America" is : it has insight,
which is a far rarer gift than the gift of observation, and I am sure that it will help
many a reader to understand things better.
I am always saying to myself and often to my
friends — I may have already repeated to so
kind a friend and reader as you — Plato's
great reminder that " the best thing we can
do for the people of a State is to make them
acquainted with each other."

When I wrote to you before, I must have
complained of being ill, and now I have the
same hindrance still, — else I should beg you
to come to see me some day very soon. I
hope, however, to stay on in town for some
little time and I am going to ask, at any rate,
that if you should be in this neighbourhood
on a winter day you will not pass the door. I
am not able yet to say that I am sure to be
equal to seeing any one at this hour or that,

— and put them to the trouble of refusal, —
but now there are many afternoons as early as
one chooses when I need not send the pleasure of a friend away, — and once within this
door I could show you many things you would
care to see!

Believe me, with my best thanks and best
wishes for a Happy New Year.

UTHERSYDE, NORTHEAST HARBOUR, MOUNT DESERT.

MY DEAR ELIZABETH, — Your note has
reached me here, and indeed, indeed I send
my most affectionate good wishes and blessing to you and Miss Marlowe. I am delighted with this plan, especially since you
are going to see Italy in summer, — so few
people do that who go travelling! You will
see the vintage coming on and the vintage
come, and so much more of the true Italy of
the poets, the out-of-door life and living
beauty that they loved, than if you had a
comfortable hotel life, keeping warm! in
early spring. I hope that you will go to little
plays in Venice, and see how many of the
old traditions live. I wish that you could
come north by Orange[1] and see a play there,

[1] In France.

and I cling to a deep desire that you should
sit in the old historic playhouse in Paris before you get back! The " Théâtre Français "
ought to belong to both of you! All this last
is n't Italy, but the card I drop into my envelope must carry you to the door of one
who knows her and loves her with the best
and most understanding love (I always in-
sist that love is n't blind : it is only love
that sees!). Miss Paget is Vernon Lee, and
you will remember her exquisite " Ariadne in
Mantua." I hope that she may be found at
home, but at any rate you will have a charming drive to the old villa just outside Flor-
ence. I shall write her about you, so that this
word on a card is very short (I can fancy Miss
Marlowe beautifully in the Ariadne!). Do
send me a word on your way, and put a twig
of olive leaves into the letter. And direct to
me at Manchester by Sea, where I expect to
be by and by.

I had a bad month with a second attack
of grippe, but I am nearly mended after a most
cheerful sailing cruise of eight days from
Portsmouth here. You can't think how good
it was to see the pointed firs and the shady
coves again and the great wide reaches of

water between the green islands. O yes, dear,
this is just the right thing, your going, and
your going together!

My sister sends you her love.

(TO MRS. HARRIET PRESCOTT SPOFFORD)

MANCHESTER BY SEA, Monday, 1908.

MY DEAR HALLY, — I have been thanking
you ever since your letter came, — you were
so good and kind to write and I loved what
you said. I found the verses among some
things I was pulling out of a desk or drawer;
I don't know in the least when they were written, but when I saw them in print I felt a
little more alive in the world. Perhaps some
day now, in the right place and with the right
kind of quietness, I shall find myself beginning all over again; but it will be a timid
young author enough! We do have our long
years' use of that strange little tool, the pen,
to fall back upon, and that must count for
something, — the wonder and uncertainty is
about a "living spring," as country people
would say, to come out of the hillside with
proper water for the ink! It was a day like
this last year that you all three came over to

Berwick, and I wish you would do it again while Annie is there. With much love and many thanks for your dear letter.

(TO MRS. FIELDS)

INTERVALE, Sunday.

Helen and I drove over to Miss Wormeley's yesterday afternoon,[1] — a wonderfully beautiful afternoon, with such high, bright clouds and such a sunset, and the view from the house of most matchless beauty. *She* was there — all her atmosphere — her books on the table, her flowers all in bloom: it was a most sad and lovely and unforgettable visit. Only on Tuesday she was there — *all day Tuesday!* it seems so wonderful, that living creature, that *friend!* I kept saying to myself those lines of Fitzgerald's in the " Agamemnon " : —

" And some light ashes in a little urn."

[1] After Miss Wormeley's death.

(TO MRS. HUMPHRY WARD AND HER
DAUGHTER)
MANCHESTER BY SEA, MASSACHUSETTS,
June 8, 1908.

DEAREST MARY AND DOROTHY, — This is
just one word of love and thanks because you
gave me the great pleasure of coming over, —
of seeing you both again! — and I feel quite
selfish about it, as if no one else could care
about seeing you and being with you again
quite so much! (This may be unjust to some
dozens of people — but never mind! You
must just take my love and blessing and believe how happy you made our dear A. F.
and me.) She is much better now than when
you saw her, the air here is always just the
right thing, and I love to see her in her little
pale grey dress sitting on the piazza looking
seaward over the green tree-tops. She *is* tired,
with getting away from Town more than from
getting here, but she will soon be rested.

I thought that you would have more days
in Quebec; I wish you could spend a week
there, — the old French country is delightful,
but you have been seeing " Country " enough.
Your dear heads will be in a whirl, between

snow mountains and the early summer heat—
I doubt if you even get time to read your letters until you begin the slow first days on
ship-board. Good-bye, good-bye! Don't you
remember that Kingsley finished his book:
"We cannot *not* have been in the West In-
dies," and so we cannot *not* have had you both
here! and *not* have had fast hold of each
other's hands again. You cannot know what
joy and delight your visit has given. I do
hope that neither of you are the worse for it.

Yours with true affection.

(TO MISS WILLA SIBERT CATHER)

MANCHESTER BY SEA, *August* 17, 1908.

MY DEAR WILLA, — I am delighted to
have your letter.

You will find that I sent a verse that I
found among my papers to "McClure's," —
and I did it as a sort of sign and warrant of
my promise to you. No story yet, but I do
not despair; I begin to dare to think that if
I could get a quiet week or two, I could really
get something done for you, and it should be
for you who gave me a "Hand up" in the
spring!

I wish that I could see you and that something might bring you to Boston and for a night to Manchester. For more than a night, or as long as you could stay. Mrs. Fields bids me say this.

I shall be here for a fortnight now, or more. It is the time of year when people crowd the foreground of every background of shore or inland life, but it is also the time for quiet days together. I wish that I could see you,— I must write the words again!

Send me one word on office paper to say that you are getting on well. I envy you your work, even with all its difficulties. I wish that I could take a handful for my own hand, and to help you.

(TO MRS. HUMPHRY WARD)

MANCHESTER BY SEA, MASSACHUSETTS,
September 1, 1908.

MY DEAR MARY,— It has been the swiftest of flights of a summer! I have been trying to solve the usual problem of trying to be in two places at once; but besides this I had two pleasant cruises down the Maine coast, of a week or so each, with Mrs. Forbes, whom you will remember; but I wish you knew the "Merlin" too, a big sailing yacht of great charm and spread of sail; and the Maine coast, since you only saw that of Southern New England, so low and quiet and different. Oh, no! you have seen the St. Lawrence region, which is more like Maine; the Pointed Firs, — the mountains near the shore; the long Norway-like fiords and islands!

I have the whole 'back of my mind' full of things that I wish to tell you, but I get so hindered about writing: not the "stop" in one's mind that Quakers gravely talk about, but something much less interesting. We are first of all so very anxious about dear Mr. Norton in these days; Sally's letters are very troubled, poor child, but she said in her last letter that she hoped to get to Mrs. Fields's for a day and night very soon. She came twice with her father to Miss Sedgwick's in the very hot weather, but unluckily I was not here. I cannot give up the hope of seeing him again. For so many reasons I am thankful that you could come last spring.

People are talking about "Diana," and those who wait for the book are finding it hard to wait. I think every one delights in it. I am waiting, too, for the book to have it *all* again, and for next month's magazine number, I must also confess! Mrs. Bell was wishing for it Saturday when she came up from the York Shore to luncheon. How I wish you had both been with her! Was the house all as you wished, and the poor hurt man doing well? We have longed to know, but I waited at first to write because I knew you would both go home to such busy days. I see that "Lady Rose" is to be played at the Castle Square Theatre, and I shall hie me to see it with great haste. I *was* so sorry that you did not have the chance in London, but you might come over to Boston! I must not write more, but to send my love. I am afraid not to seal up this poor note and send it off — next thing it will be Spring.

Yours most affectionately.

(TO MISS SARA NORTON)

SOUTH BERWICK, *September* 16, 1908.

—— I am sending a little book chiefly for the sake of its biographical preface. I have delighted in knowing Lady John Scott, and just now I have been lending her to Mrs. Bell who made friends as quickly as I did. She is such a simple and real and *dear* person. The grandniece who writes the preface must be equally nice and delightful. I thought it might be something that you and your father would like to read together. Do not hurry, or trouble to send it back, — some day I can put it in my pocket. I am going back to Manchester tomorrow or next day; these last few days I have been quite alone and have done ever so many put-off things and comforted my soul. I was much amused the other day by a tale of some good housekeeping creatures who enlivened a tea party by trying to think what they should carry with them into another world if they could choose one precious thing, — and one chirped up that she should take an empty drawer that she had in the third story. You will guess by this what turn my poor energies have taken, but indeed I have had three or four extra good days, and hope for more. I do hope that dear Mr. Norton is better and stronger too. I think a great deal about him and wish many wishes. I always forget, when I see him, to ask a question about a classmate, young Perry, whom I can just remember with deep childish affection as he was going over to Italy in '54 or

'55, — his fair hair, his amusing, kind ways to his little niece. He was my mother's brother, and died that very year abroad. I am afraid he was no student, though he studied law and had some gifts and ambitions toward political life. He was "wild," and I am afraid a little naughty, and he and Mr. Bigelow Lawrence kept each other's rather gay company.

He had been abroad before and was twenty-eight when he died. These are nearly all the things I know about him, except that I still treasure the remains of a lovely Paris paint-box that he was bringing me home. What a long story about a poor young uncle! I wonder if Susanina will preserve such memories. I must have been somewhere about five years old or a little less. He had been many months away. This Sunday I shall spend at Naushon and see the great beeches and the deer flickering about. We saw two here this summer at the edge of some woods. I had been long hoping for such a sight. Mrs. Bell came up from York for luncheon last Saturday. Was not that delightful? So well and so enchanting.

(TO MRS. HUMPHRY WARD)

MANCHESTER BY SEA,
October 1, 1908.

MY DEAR MARY, — What I most wish to
tell you is my delight in " Diana "; you have
indeed done everything to those last chapters
in making them justify Diana! They do!
They do! I have been reading again and again
with real admiration of your most noble and
beautiful gifts, — the gifts of heaven — of
sympathy and feeling and insight above all.
That defeated old Lady Lucy, with the
young strength and self - forgetful love of
Diana coming in at the door! There flits into
my mind as I write a most lovely poem of
Mr. Lowell's that begins, "How was I worthy
so divine a loss?" I think some of the lines
in it are so akin to all you felt about Oliver
and Diana, — perhaps you would not say so.
Could Oliver ever be selfish or a cad again,
with such a love? Ah, but he *was* selfish and
must so continue, and must, thank Heaven,
always be fighting and fall into worse shame
when he cannot win. And her face would be
shining more and more with the joy of watching his poor victories. My heart is full of

your story, my dear friend. I miss you so as
I write and wish that we were talking; indeed, I think we have never stopped missing
you and dear Dorothy since you went away.
Our last day, our last minutes always seem
so close.

(TO MISS SARA NORTON)

Tuesday morning, *October*, 1908.

MY DEAREST SALLY, — It was a great joy
to see your handwriting, — letters can give
such a feeling of companionship. I have been
longing for some news of your dear father,
and I was planning last week to go to town
and to Shady Hill to try to see you, but on
Monday night dear Mrs. Fields was taken very
ill, and for some days and nights I was most
anxious.

But we have begun our little pleasures, too,
and yesterday and day before I read to Mrs.
Fields awhile in Lucas's "Charles Lamb." We
have been going through the first big volume
this summer, and a chapter about all those
friends whom she knows so well seems just the
right thing. We have just got Coleridge home
from Malta, and nobody in the book or out can
think what to do with him! What wonderful

weather for us here and at Shady Hill. Last night came the first touch of frost. I see from the window that a row of zinnias are all brown, but the upper flower-bed is as bright as ever — all the friendly marigolds — and I shall have them tucked up with a blanket if it is cold again tonight. I must not write longer, but I think to you often and often with true love — you and dear Mr. Norton both. I have never been able to believe that wireless telephones were a new discovery; if you love people enough you can be your own battery, the only thing is to teach us how to use it, — so often it seems to go off by accident only. What a scientific turn this letter takes! but never mind; it carries you much love and many wishes.

(TO MR. DAVID DOUGLAS)

MANCHESTER BY SEA, MASS., *October* 20.

MY DEAR MR. DOUGLAS, — Day after day has gone by, warm and misty or rather smoky from the great forest fires that have so afflicted the country east and west. We are apt to have a wet, windy October and nearly all November like this, but it has been an unusual summer in many respects, hardly any

rain and yet little real drought. The farmers,
who do not often dig their wells deep enough,
are always afraid of the ground's freezing before the great rains come, and having to drive
their poor cattle far to water, but let us hope
that all the springs will fill in season this
year. We have seen Mr. and Mrs. Bryce lately
— since their return from England. [The Em-
bassy has had its summer quarters almost
on the next place] and the Ambassador seems
to feel little uneasiness about high affairs on
either side the Atlantic. They are now away,
so that we don't know how the latest affairs
in Turkey, etc., affect his mind. He is a delightful man. Nobody could be more welcome
to either his place of State or to his old friends
in America. I have been wishing to ask you
if it would be possible to find a copy of
"Gleanings from an Old Portfolio," edited by
Mrs. Godfrey Clark? I see that it was pri-
vately printed, but sometimes such a book
comes into the market. I was reminded of it
by the list at the head of a paper in the July
"Quarterly Review" about my favorite Lady
Louisa Stuart. I always thank you for giving
me the pleasure of what has been a true
"book friendship." This year I have lost

one of my dearest older friends, Miss Katharine Wormeley, who was of the Lady Louisa ("guinea!") stamp and rank, a delightful "great lady," — daughter of an American mother and an English admiral, who fought in the Peninsular Wars, and was already retired when his younger children were born. Miss Wormeley had seen much of the world all her days, but her last years were spent in a quiet house among our "White Mountains," where she busied herself with French translations, Balzac, etc., being wise enough to know that a hermit should not be idle! She lived as if she lived in London, but for months she heard few sounds beside the wind and the mountain brooks and the foxes barking on the hills. I delight in the thought of my visits to her. Lately I have been re-reading the preface of the "Lady John Scott," and delighting in it more than ever. Has "Margaret Warrender" who signs it written other things? — for this preface is a very uncommon piece of writing of that difficult and delicate sort.

For how many pleasures I have to thank you, dear Mr. Douglas! and I must beg for one more; that we may hear from you soon and have good news of you and all your household. I hope that Miss Douglas will be happening on a new sketching ground; her work is so interesting and must provide you with many treasures and souvenirs.

(TO MISS WILLA SIBERT CATHER)

SOUTH BERWICK, Friday, 27th *November*, 1908.

MY DEAR WILLA, — I was glad to get your letter last night, and I was sorry to miss the drive to the station and a last talk about the story and other things; but I was too tired — "spent quite bankrupt!" It takes but little care about affairs, and almost less true pleasure, to make me feel overdone, and I have to be careful — it is only stupid and disappointing, but *there it is*, as an old friend of mine often says dolefully. And I knew that I was disappointing you, besides disappointing and robbing myself, which made it all the harder. It would have been such a good piece of a half hour! Emerson was very funny once, Mrs. Fields has told me, when he said to a friend, "You formerly bragged of ill-health, sir!" But indeed I don't brag, I only deplore and often think it is a tiresome sort of mortification. I begin to think this is just what makes

old age so trying to many persons. It seemed
a very long little journey, and I could hardly
sit up in my place in the car. I have never
been very strong, but always capable of "great
pulls."

I expect to be here until Monday the seventh,
unless dear Mrs. Fields should need me. I
have just had a most dear and cheerful note
from her, and we spoke by telephone last evening. She wrote me about the pink roses.

And now I wish to tell you — the first of
this letter being but a preface — with what
deep happiness and recognition I have read the
"McClure" story, — night before last I found
it with surprise and delight. It made me feel
very near to the writer's young and loving
heart. You have drawn your two figures of
the wife and her husband with unerring touches
and wonderful tenderness for her. It makes
me the more sure that you are far on your
road toward a fine and long story of very high
class. The lover is as well done as he could be
when a woman writes in the man's character,
— it must always, I believe, be something of
a masquerade. I think it is safer to write
about him as you did about the others, and
not try to be he! And you could almost have

done it as yourself — a woman could love her
in that same protecting way — a woman could
even care enough to wish to take her away
from such a life, by some means or other.
But oh, how close — how tender — how true
the feeling is! the sea air blows through the
very letters on the page. Do not hurry too
fast in these early winter days, — a quiet hour
is worth more to you than anything you can
do in it.

148 Charles Street, BOSTON, MASS.,
Sunday, 13th of *December.*

MY DEAR WILLA, — I have been thinking
about you and hoping that things are going
well. I cannot help saying what I think about
your writing and its being hindered by such
incessant, important, responsible work as you
have in your hands now. I do think that it is
impossible for you to work so hard and yet have
your gifts mature as they should — when one's
first working power has spent itself nothing
ever brings it back just the same, and I do
wish in my heart that the force of this very
year could have gone into three or four
stories. In the " Troll - Garden " the Sculp-
tor's Funeral stands alone a head higher than

the rest, and it is to that level you must hold and take for a starting-point. You are older now than that book in general; you have been living and reading and knowing new types; but if you don't keep and guard and mature your force, and above all, have time and quiet to perfect your work, you will be writing things not much better than you did five years ago. This you are anxiously saying to yourself! but I am wondering how to get at the right conditions. I want you to be surer of your backgrounds, — you have your Nebraska life, — a child's Virginia, and now an intimate knowledge of what we are pleased to call the "Bohemia" of newspaper and magazine-office life. These are uncommon equipment, but you don't see them yet quite enough from the outside, — you stand right in the middle of each of them when you write, without having the standpoint of the looker-on who takes them each in their relations to letters, to the world. Your good schooling and your knowledge of "the best that has been thought and said in the world," as Matthew Arnold put it, have helped you, but these you wish and need to deepen and enrich still more. You must find a quiet place near the best companions (not those who admire and wonder at everything one does, but those who know the good things with delight!). You do need reassurance, — every artist does! — but you need still more to feel "responsible for the state of your conscience" (your literary conscience, we can just now limit that quotation to), and you need to dream your dreams and go on to new and more shining ideals, to be aware of "the gleam" and to follow it; your vivid, exciting companionship in the office must not be your audience, you must find your own quiet centre of life, and write from that to the world that holds offices, and all society, all Bohemia; the city, the country — in short, you must write to the human heart, the great consciousness that all humanity goes to make up. Otherwise what might be strength in a writer is only crudeness, and what might be insight is only observation; sentiment falls to sentimentality — you can write about life, but never write life itself. And to write and work on this level, we must live on it — we must at least recognize it and defer to it at every step. We must be ourselves, but we must be our

best selves. If we have patience with cheapness and thinness, as Christians must, we
must know that it *is* cheapness and not make
believe about it. To work in silence and with
all one's heart, that is the writer's lot; he is
the only artist who must be a solitary, and
yet needs the widest outlook upon the world.
But you have been growing I feel sure in the
very days when you felt most hindered, and
this will be counted to you. You need to have
time to yourself and time to read and add
to your recognitions. I do not know when a
letter has grown so long and written itself so
easily, but I have been full of thought about
you. You will let me hear again from you
before long?

(TO MISS FRANCES MORSE)

Friday afternoon [*January* 23, 1909].

DEAREST FANNY, — I have just been to
Berwick for a few days, and I thought I
should certainly write to you, and then I
did n't! I don't often have one of the days
when I could n't do anything *but* write, —
but this five minutes seems quite unaccounta-
bly to be mine this first afternoon in town. I

have wished to ask you if you have seen or
would care to see a new story of Mr. James's
— "The Jolly Corner" (it is a corner and was
once jolly). There are lovely things in it and
a wonderful analysis of fear in the dark, so
that it may please you better by day than by
night, as it did me! I have been reading over
again, too, Vernon Lee's "Hortus Vitæ," and
wondering if that were the book of hers that
we talked about last year; it is the one with
the lovely dedication to Madame Blanc-Bentzon.

I chiefly wish to tell you about a drive yesterday " down the other side of the river ";
the river frozen (the tide-river I mean now);
the snow very white and thinly spread like
nicest frosting over the fields, and the pine
woods as black as they could be, — no birds,
but the tracks of every sort of little beastie.
They seemed to have been *all out* on visits
and errands and going *such* distances on their
little paws and claws; somehow it looks too
much for a mouse to go half a mile along the
road or across a field. Think how a hawk
would see him! I think we knew every track
but one, — it had long claws like a crow's and
a tail that never lifted; — we settled upon a

big old rat who had come up from an old wharf
by the river-side.

Dear Fanny, I do so hope that you are getting stronger; being sick is fun compared to
getting well, as dear Mr. Warner used to say.
Do take long enough; I have had such drear
times trying to play well when I *wasn't!*

And so the letters went on, with the flickering lights and shadows of human life re-
flected on their pages, until she wrote one day
in June, 1909: " Dear, I do not know what to
do with me! " Then hope died; we knew she
could no longer stay with us, for like a little
child, she had always planned some pretty
scheme to cheer the paths of others, as well as
her own, when the way was difficult. She rested
on the spirit within her, which was not of herself, and dared with a fearlessness that did
not think on daring. She never put her doll
away and always used her child-names, but
her plans were large and sometimes startling
to others. To herself her plans were joy-
ous, every difficult time in life being met with
a fine ingenuity of resource, until at the last

she sent the little plaintive cry, "I do not know what to do with me!" Then she was borne away from these human trammels and her young soul was free to move in the atmosphere of Divine Love.

INDEX

𝔗𝔥𝔢 𝔕𝔦𝔳𝔢𝔯𝔰𝔦𝔡𝔢 𝔓𝔯𝔢𝔰𝔰

CAMBRIDGE . MASSACHUSETTS

U . S . A